turn of the century
# THE GROUP

*turn of* **the** *century*

# THE GROUP

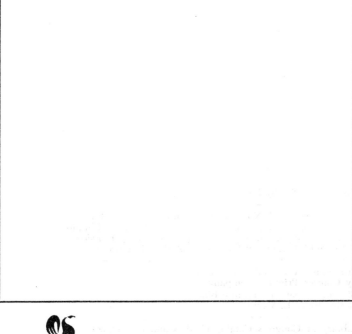

**PHOENIX PUBLISHING** •     Canaan, New Hampshire 03741

Printed in the United States of America
by Courier Printing Company
Binding by New Hampshire Bindery
Design by A. L. Morris

Library of Congress Catalog Card Number 73-88324
ISBN 0-914016-02-4

_turn of the century_
# THE GROUP

## INTRODUCTION

"Granny, did you fart?"

Torn from the perusal of the memoires of Vassar 1902, I regarded my enchanting three year old granddaughter.

"No, Alison, Granny didn't f - - -," I couldn't bring myself to use that word which had joined my vocabulary as recently as my own college years. "It was this chair." I swung it around, producing the same small muffled explosion. "Please go find your mother now, and have your nap. Afterwards maybe we'll go out in the boat."

Always running, she left the room, slamming the door; but quickly opened it again.

"Granny, I guess the chair farted!" She banged the door.

Shaken with laughter, I returned to the four shoe boxes of letters on my desk. When _my_ mother, then Fanny Simpson, was at Vassar, she wrote to _her_ mother with amazing frequency. A generation later, when I was at Vassar, a telegram or collect phone call home was par for the course.

Before settling down again to my job of sorting and editing these letters, I ruminated about the great savoir faire plus the lack of contemporary surface sophistication of my mother. I'm sure that *fart* was never in her personal lexicon. I was reminded of a recent family dinner party at Passy in New York. My paternal Aunt Louise, ten years younger than Mother, had told a story.

"A baby was born with a smile upon his face. One hand was tightly clenched. The doctor thought this odd. He opened up the little fist, and there was the pill." We all laughed politely.

"What pill?" burst forth Mother. "What do you mean *the* pill? Why do you tell such obscure jokes, Louise?" Mother was vexed, and her voice carried to surrounding tables, causing smiles and even quiet laughs. We all roared.

Back at my task, I realized that many of these letters from Vassar were concerned with social life, week-end plans, and fashion. I'm sure this did not mean that college had no other values for my mother. She was a member of Phi Beta Kappa, and for the last part of her life (she died in her ninetieth year), was president of the class of 1902.

Each individual reading these letters is aware, at least to some extent, of what goes on in the colleges and in the world today. But few have the opportunity of knowing the personal experiences of an undergraduate group at the turn of the century; and for this reason, I do not question the validity of preserving these letters.

Edgartown, Massachusetts
July 1971

*turn of the century*
# THE GROUP

## THE SIMPSON HERITAGE

"One of the most distinguished men in the music trade is Mr. John Boulton Simpson, the millionaire, who has for years been president of the Estey Piano Company. Mr. Simpson is not only a wealthy man, but a very enterprising man, and has used his means in a number of worthy business ventures, among them being one of the largest and finest hotels on Lake George; but never mind how much enterprise Mr. Simpson might display, however well he might invest his means and use his time as a promoter of valuable business undertakings, he would not obtain one line of notice from any one of the daily papers. But the other day, when his footman took a party of guests, in his private omnibus, to the Waldorf-Astoria to supper, while Mr. and Mrs. Simpson followed in a private hansom, and it happened while the party were taking supper that a truck driver got into a row with Mr. Simpson's coachman and had a fight which resulted in the coachman's arrest and Mr. Simpson appearing in the station-house to bail him out, every daily paper in the city had a report, and as Mr. Simpson, being compelled to give real estate bail, gave his $200,000 mansion on Fifth Avenue as security, that was an additional reason for flaming headlines.

"What nonsense all this is! Why cannot the daily papers find something better to fill their columns, than stuff that can only appeal to the lowest intelligence?"

Thus was described the father of my mother, Fanny Proddow Simpson (Townsend), in the November 30th, 1901 issue of the weekly magazine, *Music Traders.*

John Simpson of Lodore, Cumberland County, England (1747-1816) married Mary Youdale (1749-1810). John and Mary had sons and grandsons who came to New York City early in the 19th century and were the first in that city to engage in the pawnbroking business. These statistics come mainly from family records compiled by Fanny Simpson Townsend (Vassar College, 1902), the great-great-granddaughter of John Simpson. The entire Simpson family genealogy has been painstakingly researched by William P. Harris, Jr., also a descendant of John Simpson, and incidentally the father of America's famous actress, Julie Harris.

Much detailed family history has been compiled and published in the book, *Hockshop,* by William Rooe Simpson and his wife, Florence K. Simpson, with Charles Samuels, published in 1951 by Random House.

One of John Simpson's progeny, William (alias Walter Stevenson), was born in England and died in New York City in 1847. According to Hockshop he was a goldsmith in London and came to New York in 1822. Here he used the alias "Walter Stevenson" because he was allegedly threatened by creditors who were close to King George IV of England. William Simpson opened his business at 25 Chatham Street, later called Park Row. He lived here with his housekeeper as common-

2

law wife and raised a family of eleven children.

None of William's sons went into the pawnbroking business and as trade flourished he sent for four of his nephews. These young men were eventually taken into the firm and later left to open their own pawnshops, each destined to become a millionaire.

The word "uncle" which dictionaries still include as the slang for pawnbroker, originated when the nephews were working for their relative. During their apprenticeship, whenever a customer offered unusual collateral they would politely tell him, "I'll have to ask my uncle."

To support the four young pawnbrokers, the hockshop business had to be good, and it was. Although the Simpson pawnshops catered to those who frequented the Bowery, lending them money for drink, the bums actually contributed only a very small part of their income. The numerous Simpson men took in pawn over the years rare prints, heirlooms and family jewels, old masters and even a Stradivarius. Following the tragic kidnap of Charles A. Lindbergh, Jr., in 1932, the 44½ carat Hope diamond was exchanged by Mrs. Evalyn Walsh McLean of Washington, D.C. for pawn tickets and $100,000 in cash to pay the kidnap ransom.

It is not the purpose of this book to trace the confusing background of the many Simpsons who made the family both wealthy and famous in their trade. Fanny Simpson's grandfather, William Simpson, Jr., joined his uncle Walter Stevenson in the Park Row hockshop. When the property was sold for the western approach to the Brooklyn Bridge at a price of $157,000, Simpson used this with other savings and invested heavily in real estate and public utilities. With his brother, John Bolton Simpson, he purchased 132 acres of land in the West Farms or Hunts Point section of what is now the Bronx. According to the authors of *Hockshop*, to cross the lands the brothers once owned, today one would have to ride seven stations on the elevated line.

3

Most of the Simpsons drank in moderation but one exotic character resented the fact that his hockshop duties interfered with his boozing. Obsessed with the fear that he might starve to death, he purchased a large Canadian estate, and hired a hundred trappers, hunters and fishermen to obtain a huge stock of fish and game. After they had filled the big refrigeration plant Simpson built on his property, he contentedly returned to his drinking, forgot to eat, and died of starvation!

Another Simpson who used between $100,000 and $200,-000 of his earnings to keep and breed horses, was persuaded by his son to sell some of his animals. At the last moment he changed his mind and instructed his agent to attend the auction and buy them back. This change of mind cost the business $17,300 for the auctioneer's fee. This same Simpson bought a large stable in Lexington, Kentucky. He also built indoor and outdoor tracks on Simpson's Empire City Farms in Cuba, New York. To provide enough fodder for the horses he kept there he acquired twenty-seven farms. It was said that it cost him between $3,000 and $4,000 a month just to feed his horses!

Fanny's father, John Boulton Simpson, Jr. was born in 1846 at 121st Street and the East River. After attending the Collegiate School on 14th Street and Sixth Avenue, he naturally worked in *his* father's hockshop. Some years after his marriage he spent most of his time at the Estey Piano Company, his father having helped him purchase a controlling interest. With this badge of respectability he proceeded to develop the Lake George area, was president of the Sagamore Hotel Company, and built a summer home on Bolton Landing adjacent to his hotel. A veteran of the 7th Regiment, New York Volunteers, he was accepted for membership in the Union League, Columbia Yacht, the New York Athletic and Lake George clubs.

In 1872 John Simpson married Frances Collins Shilton, the daughter of Joseph P. Shilton and his wife Frances Proddow (whose mother was a sister of his grandmother, Sarah Simpson). Fanny's mother, Frances, was one of eight children

4

who became orphaned when both parents died of pneumonia within two days. Of necessity the children were divided and Fanny's mother was adopted by her distant cousin, William Simpson. In 1867 she graduated from the Girls Grammar School Number 47 on Twelfth Street.

Frances Shilton became a school teacher, one of the few respectable occupations open to women in that day. When John Boulton Simpson, Jr. courted and proposed to his Fanny, it was said that she refused to marry him until she had earned enough money teaching school so that she could educate her sister, Esther. Once this goal was realized she consented to the marriage but it was not long before she told her husband and others that to her the family's pawnbroking business was an anathema. Since their family now included two small daughters, it was understandable that she might have had social ambitions for them — as well as herself and her husband.

In time she won her point whereupon her husband's father helped him buy the American agency of the Estey Piano Company. To Frances this was a much more dignified and socially acceptable business, but the rest of the family was scornful of such snobbery and promptly nicknamed her husband "Piano Johnny."

Fanny Simpson's mother was actively interested in many charities. Between running almost daily errands for her own daughter Fan while she was at Vassar, she served as treasurer for more than twenty-eight years of St. Andrew's Guild, the women's organization of that church, and was manager of the St. Luke's Home for aged women.

One of the societies to which she belonged was known as Garland Luncheons. According to the printed program for the January 30, 1897 meeting, her table was decorated as follows:

"Three garlands of flowering smilax down the center of table, with garlands hanging from each corner, fastened with large green satin bows. Chandelier was garlanded also. An ornamental centerpiece composed of four horns of plenty filled

with candied fruits. Flowers in slender vases at each end of the table. The beautiful decorations were carried out at each cover by large bunches of appropriate flowers and souvenir cards."
The menu was not for slimming:
"Courses —
1st — raw oysters
2nd — soup
3rd — fish croquettes, tartare sauce
4th —  quail on toast served with peas and potato croquettes
5th — shrimp salad
6th — sponge pudding with hard sauce
7th — tortoni cream, in pretty souvenir boxes
8th — coffee, bonbons, salted nuts galore
One of the novelties of this pretty luncheon was the butter in forms of baskets holding small balls of butter.
Champagne."

Such was the family background of Fanny Proddow Simpson, who was born in 1881 and her younger sister Helen, or "The Kid," as Fanny affectionately referred to her. It was only natural that in her spending habits the second Fanny should follow the example of her ever generous mother, her occasional imperious manner, and her desire to do the right thing socially at all times. Perhaps it was from the Simpson side of the family that she received those other traits which endeared her to her many friends — a spontaneous gaiety, a gregarious instinct, genuine generosity, and a sense of responsibility to help those who were less fortunate than herself.

# THE GROUP

*turn of the century*

## BEFORE COLLEGE

Fanny Simpson attended Miss Annie Brown's School in New York. Occasionally she boarded, but most of the time commuted from her home in Harlem at 11 Mt. Morris Park West, where the Simpsons lived until their move to Fifth Avenue.

The headlines in the New York Journal on Thursday, November 5th, 1896, were not so very different from many headlines appearing in the late nineteen sixties.

"M'KINLEY GIRLS' MIDNIGHT PRANKS

HAVE FUN WITH BRYAN MAIDS AT MISS BROWN'S
    SWELL SCHOOL

DESCEND A FIRE ESCAPE TO SERENADE SIX
    SOUTHERN SILVER PATRIOTS

THEIR FUN RESENTED, AND IN SCANTY ATTIRE,

## THEY ARE DRENCHED WITH ICE COLD WATER

## ONE VICTIM DEMANDS REDRESS, IT NOT BEING IMMEDIATELY FORTHCOMING, SHE PACKS HER TRUNKS AND HAS GONE WITH HER MOTHER TO THE LATTER'S HOTEL

When Miss Brown returns to her Fifth avenue school she will probably be told that the election of Major McKinley as President has been properly looked after. The celebration, unfortunately, was marred by one of Mrs. Wood's young women getting offended, and her mother taking her away. Whether the retirement is to be permanent will appear later. All Mrs. Frances Fisher Wood, A.B. (Vassar) head of the day school, is prepared to admit is that the young woman has gone with her mother to recover from nervousness.

It would be manifestly unfair to refer to the election night episode as a college hazing, for such a thing could not happen at Miss Brown's, where the daughters of the rich are prepared for Vassar. As Mrs. Wood says, it was only a bit of campaign fun. Mrs. Wood regrets the occurrence as much as anyone could who is charged with the responsibility of nurturing and training so many blooming buds of womanhood.

As Mrs. Wood talked of the unfortunate affair, the girl who had been offended stood in the front hall with her mother, and on the floor above them were the bags and packing cases containing the young woman's effects. They were going to a hotel to stop for a few days. Mrs. Wood did her best to arrange matters, but was only partly successful.

Mrs. Wood could not be tempted to give any of the names. She referred to the girl as 'Rita', said she was a Southern bred young woman, and that her father had dropped dead two years ago from heart disease. Since then the daughter had been very nervous, and had been treated for it with electricity.

## HER SPECIAL PULLMAN

When anything happens at Miss Brown's School, it becomes important because it happens to important persons. The last thing to happen was the marriage of one of the pupils, a daughter of George M. Pullman, and then Mrs. Wood had a special Pullman car all to herself and went to the wedding in high state.

Miss Brown's School has but one rival, and that is Miss Ely's on the Riverside Drive. At Miss Brown's each girl pays $1,000, and she occupies a room with two others, a dainty single bed being prepared for each. There are fees for extras, such as being trained in the Choral Club by Walter Damrosch, or in singing by Mrs. Garrit Smith.

The chaperonage is perfect, including the morning walk in the park and during the attendance of the male music teachers. No school in America has such a list of patrons. It includes these names: Seth Low of Columbia, J. Pierpont Morgan of Wall Street, the Rev. Robert Collyer, the Rev. Edward Everett Hale of Boston, Mrs. Mary Mapes Dodge of St. Nicholas, Smith M. Weed the Plattsburg statesman, John W. Harper, General D. N. Flagler U.S.A., George M. Pullman, ex-Governor Roswell P. Flower, William C. Whitney, and Bishop Potter.

It can, with this patronage, easily be imagined that a majority of the girl students are Republican in their sympathies. Indeed, there are only a half dozen Bryan patriots among the forty dormitory pupils, and they are from the South. Among those was Rita. Her classmates say she was — and is — in full sympathy with the ambitions of the Nebraska orator and statesman, and a believer in the beneficent effects of a free and unlimited silver coinage. Among her Southern friends in the school are Miss Winnie Burgh, Miss Langhorn, sister-in-law of Charles Dana Gibson, the artist, and a Miss Proudfit of Memphis.

## WANTED ELECTION RETURNS

As Mrs. Wood tells the story, the girls were so eager for election returns that they begged her to go to the Barnard Club, or if that was impossible, to buy them some newspapers. They could not go out, for 9.30 o'clock was marked by the sounding of the gong that meant 'lights out.'

Mrs. Wood did not get back till that hour had passed, and then she found ten of her young ladies engaged in a novel torchlight parade. They had lighted candles, and were marching up and down the halls.

Here Mrs. Wood ceases to relate the story. She will not go beyond the torchlight parade and confess that there was some innocent fun beyond, about which she cannot speak until she has first told the facts to Miss Brown on her return.

The girls most interested in the proceedings are not saying a word, but among the day scholars, whose homes line Fifth avenue, the facts were rolled over and over yesterday, and proved the sensation of the school day.

It would not be best to reproduce the story as told by one of these young women under quotation marks. In substance it was:

For days before the election the dormitory girls had been laying in a stock of candles for a torchlight parade. They resented the fervid patriotism of the Bryan girls, six in number, but not until the returns began to come in, through the six little colored 'buttons' sent out before Mrs. Wood's return, did they contemplate such a celebration as developed.

In their 'nighties' and bathroom slippers they paraded through the long halls, each big enough to contain a Harlem flat. In front of the doors of the rooms occupied by the Bryan girls they executed a mock serenade. In the midst of the fun Mrs. Wood returned, and promptly ordered them to their rooms in another house of the four used by the school.

## MORE FUN NECESSARY

After consultation it was decided to keep up the fun, even

10

to the extent of breaking their way back into the house from which they had been ejected. The only way to do it was by the fire escape, which leads from floor to floor in the rear, but in full view of part of Fifty-sixth street, now occupied happily by John Jacob Astor's unfinished flats.

They were still in their muslin gowns and slippers, and the night was chill. They put on bath robes and began the perilous descent. The iron steps were narrow and cold, and they had to go one at a time down three floors till the proper window was reached to give entrance to the hall where their victims were, presumably by this time sound asleep.

They resumed the serenade, and in a few minutes the six irate Southern girls opened their doors, and then there was fun. Just what happened no one who absolutely knows will tell, but the story told by the day scholars is that the Southern girls' rooms were sacked, all the bureau drawers being emptied in the middle of the floor, and the beds turned upside down and inside out.

The fun went fast and furious, till finally patience ceasing to be a virtue, Rita grabbed a big pitcher of water and emptied it over the crowd of tormentors, wetting them so thoroughly that in the chill night air they were glad to give up the fight and sneak back up to their beds by way of the cold fire escape.

Miss Rita was furious. After breakfast yesterday, she went to Mrs. Wood and repeated the details, expressing her opinion of her treatment at the hands of the McKinleyites, and declaring that if she couldn't get satisfaction, she would go home with her mother, who had been lingering at a hotel in town since the opening of the fall term on October first.

It is said Mrs. Wood tried her best to placate her and smooth over the trouble, declaring that for the good of her country she ought to be willing to overlook what was meant only as fun. Miss Rita refused to be patriotic to that extent, and finally, the scholars say, Mrs. Wood said she didn't see how she could do anything further, but that she would be

11

glad to have her defer her departure until Miss Brown's return, so that the latter could act in the premises.

The young woman's Southern blood was up, and she would promise nothing further than to communicate with her mother regarding what had happened, feeling sure that she would not submit to anything less than ample reparation and an apology for what had happened.

The mother called and the packing up in the afternoon was the outcome.

Miss Brown, by her unusual tact, may be able to heal the girl's bruised spirit so that she will consent to return, but last night she stopped at her mother's hotel.

Miss Brown's School is at nos. 711, 713, 715, and 717 Fifth avenue, across the way from Dr. John Hall's church, and within a stone's throw of the Cornelius Vanderbilt and Collis P. Huntington mansions. The school is like a home. Each girl has a tea table in her room, and five o'clocks are as common as caucuses on the East Side. On the dining table there are supplies of milk, crackers and apples all the day long so that no appetite shall remain unappeased for even the shortest possible moment."

In the Spring of 1898, Fanny was a boarder at Miss Brown's.

---

715 Fifth Avenue
April 26

Dearest Mother,

Do send me some clothes. Either my turquoise blue or my yellow and my gray felt hat. Most of the girls are going to wear high neck organdies on Friday. I wish my white organdie was finished. What on earth shall I wear? I think I would like to wear my old white low neck dress. When my white shirt waist is washed, I want it. You and Papa must come to the fair. I have not given a single thing to the fair.

If you can find anything nice for a college table, do send it. I am getting along splendidly here.

Love to all.

Yours affectionately,<br>Fan

---

715 Fifth Avenue<br>May 4

Well, my poor dear little Mother, what did you go get sick for anyway? I certainly am sorry for you.

The school is quite excited now because some of the girls, Carlotta Hart and Manira Simpson in particular, the two handsomest girls in school, have found their best dresses, which have been hanging up in closets, covered with ink and cut and slashed into. Somebody evidently has a grudge against them.

Guess who was here tonight, took dinner with Miss Brown and talked to the girls afterwards. Mrs. Wentworth, your old physical culture teacher. She remembered me and asked after you.

I have changed my room, for the present at least, and am now rooming on the third floor with Florence Delabarre.

Adele Neustadt sails for Europe next Tuesday. We the senior class are trying to arrange to see her off. Isn't it too bad she can't graduate with us. I think her sister is the selfishest thing. Mrs. N. is sailing on Tuesday, Mr. N. on the 2nd of June. Adele's sister won't leave the gayeties of N.Y. until the 2nd, so of course, Adele has to go with her mother.

Goodnight, dearest, don't get sick any more.

Lovingly,<br>Fan

---

715 Fifth Avenue<br>May 8

Miss Brown wants to send out the invitations to the commencement and dance right away. I will probably have about eight or nine invitations I can send to people I think will come for the afternoon, and about seven to send to those I know won't come. I have about ten invitations for the dance. (*Surprising to have such a stag line in those days!*) Now whom shall I ask? First about the dance. I suggest:

Theo McGraw

Chad Elmer

Arthur Van de Water

Ray Sawyer, if I can find his address

Jack Howe

Harry Fisher, only I never see him in the winter

What about the Roselle youths, Charlie, Louis, Gene, Waldo and Dick. I don't think I'll ask them but — Oh, dear do help me. Whom shall I ask?

To commencement in the afternoon people who will come: you and Papa of course. Be sure to tell Papa that he must make no engagement for Friday afternoon, May 27th. The three Aunts, I suppose. Will Howe perhaps. Oh, I don't know whom I ought to invite. And as for the people I *know* won't come —

Now dearest Mumsie, do send me a list immediately, for the three kinds of invitations, also the people's addresses.

Love to Papa and the kid (her younger sister, Helen) and other relatives.

Lovingly,

Fan

*Apparently Fanny had no dearth of beaux, and possibly no compunction in how she treated them. I'm sure that Mr. Torrey would not have accepted an invitation to the dance.*

---

Windsor Hotel

Montreal, Canada

Sept. 20, '97

My dear Miss Simpson,

After great deliberation I have decided to send back the

14

Browns pin you gave me to wear. My main reason is the way in which you have treated me and on account of that it will be impossible for me to oblige you by wearing it longer. I remain

Yours truly,
T. D. Torrey
715 Fifth Avenue
May 26

---

Dearest Darlingest Mother and Father,

Well of all beautiful things, mine are the beautifullyest! Thank you lots and *lots* and LOTS. I will kiss and hug you for them to-morrow. The watch and pin, the chatelaine, the hand-kerchiefs and Aunty Smith's fan, all are beautiful. Please my dear Mother I have found out that we have a rehearsal tomorrow at ten sharp. Could you tell her not to come until 10.30, or can I keep her waiting half an hour.

Love, love, love and kisses, kisses, kisses for you both from your eldest lovingest daughter,

Fan

P.S. As for being just exactly what I wanted, well I don't know.

*In spite of being a student in good standing at Miss Brown's , Fanny had to go to Poughkeepsie in 1897 and 1898 to take entrance exams for Vassar.*

---

Poughkeepsie, N. Y.
June 2

Dearest Mother,

I have been very busy ever since I arrived here. So I know you will forgive me for not writing you last night. We arrived safely yesterday after a hot and dusty trip. I have a very nice room right next to Miss Chater. Today I took my Latin and English exams. The Latin was easy, but the Eng-lish was hard and I am very doubtful. I found out the dis-

15

tribution of rooms to the freshmen is not made until September. I will ask for a room in Strong Hall.

Goodnight dear, lots of love. Don't forget to write me about trains and whether I am to wait at Garrison or go to the hotel.

Fan

---

West Point Hotel<br>West Point, N. Y.

Dearest Mother,

I heard about my two hardest exams. Greek and English. I passed them both. The English Professor said that there were very few papers better than mine. Wasn't that fine? The other exams I haven't heard about yet.

Thank you very much for the veils, gloves, hosiery, hairpin, ribbons etc. you put in. There are lots of things I want but as you are not going to bring a trunk, I suppose I can get along all right without. I want a white piqué skirt, my gingham string neck ties, my white leghorn hat but never mind about that, my red leather and tan leather belt, another white or light blue organdie dress. And you forgot to put in my new black patent leather slippers. I had to wear my very old ones Saturday night as I did not want to wear white ones. There is a hop Friday night. I can't wear my purple organdie low neck on account of the sleeves. Do bring up some interesting fiction and if you have room *Cupid and Croesus,* and *The Documents in Evidence,* I think they are in my desk or book case.

Now never mind about all these things, dear. I am going walking, so good-bye.

Fan, with love

*Fanny was accepted at Vassar, and went there happily in the fall of 1898. However, during her senior year at Miss Brown's her imagination ran rampant, and one of her compositions proved that sometimes she entertained other ideas.*

# COURT

I don't think I ever began to live until I was about eighteen years old. It was my last year in a fashionable boarding school.

One day just after lessons were finished a teacher came into my room holding up a yellow envelope. It contained these words: "Come at once, failed in business, Mother very ill, Father." Of course I packed as quickly as possible and left for home that night.

For the next month I nursed my mother steadily and she finally recovered, but it was plain that this climate was the worst possible for her health, so my father set about trying to get a position somewhere else. At last he succeeded. It was farther away than he wished, being in South America, but it was the best obtainable.

A few days after this a letter came from my uncle who was American Minister to Spain, asking me to live with him for the three or four years my mother and father expected to be in South America. It was an opportunity not to be lost, two or three years in a foreign court. And then the economy, for of course my uncle, who was a very rich man, would pay all my expenses for the time I lived with him.

I had great ambition and wished to be considered the most highly educated and most brilliant conversationalist of all the ladies in court. I must have all the accomplishments, ease, grace and manners of a court lady and not disgrace my relatives.

To think of being presented to the King and the Queen Regent! And then my court dress! I thought the best place to be when you were separated from your family was in court.

My cousin, a girl of about my own age, had just been presented at court. Though I had only seen her a couple of times in my life I loved her dearly, and felt that she would keep me from being homesick more than anybody.

We were to start in six months, and as that was not a very

long time in which to prepare for three or four years, we had to hurry, so I did not have much time to be homesick. Of course I had my wardrobe to get ready, which was not very large. And then I took quite a few books as I imagined it must be dull sometimes even in court.

# turn of the century
# THE GROUP

## FRESHMAN YEAR

*Unless otherwise noted all of the following letters were written at Vassar College, Poughkeepsie, New York.*

---

September 26, 1898

Dearest Mother,

I do want to set your mind at rest by telling you that I am beautifully fixed. I like Florence Benedict very much, and am pleased with my room. Of course I am not the least bit settled yet but I will be as soon as possible. The principal thing I want now is a chiffoneir (or however you spell it) so I am going to try to get one soon, and then I can unpack my trunk. Do bring me the largest white birch bark trash basket you can find.

Please don't worry about me because I am not nearly as

homesick as I was. Even when I went to bed last night I was not blue. I moved my bed close up to Florence's and slept well. We have some very nice girls near us and I am much more cheerful about myself.

I have numerous letters to write so au revoir, dearest. Do kiss Helen and Papa for me.

Ever your loving,
Fan

---

September 27

Dearest Sweetest Mamsie,

I love you! I love you! I love you! I do! What would I not give if I could be with you now but I can't so I am going to be as cheerful as I can. I got twelve letters this morning, two from Edythe Fraser, one from Aunt Esther, one from Arthur Hyde, one from Frances, one from Helen Halsey, three from Papa, one from the kid and one from my dearest little Mother. Do hug and kiss Helen and Papa for me.

I am not yet unpacked as we have begun recitations and I have not a minute. Hard! Mammy dear, you have no idea what they are like. Please I do not need to come back next year if I don't want to, do I? I ought to be studying now. Please don't expect too much of me, there's a dear.

From your most mostest loving daughter,
Fan

---

October 3

Darlingest Mamsie

Here I am back at Vassar once more. When the train reached Tarrytown I looked out to see if Bessy would get on, but she didn't nor did she get on at Sing Sing. So I had to come all the way by myself. We were on time when we got to Garrison, but shortly after we left there the train stopped still for about an hour so we did not get into Poughkeepsie until about 6.15, when of course it was pitch dark. I got some coffee at the station and then of course got on a trolley car that was not "through" and would not transfer me. So out I got at Market Street and waited for a "through" car. I got out here just in time for chapel. I found two letters from Aunt Esther; one was an answer to a crazy note I wrote her about hating it here, etc. It was the funniest letter you ever read. When you see her do give her my love.

I must study, unpack etc.

Your mostest loving,
Fan

---

October 4

Dearest Mamsie,

Please write a letter to Mrs. Kendrick saying that I may have callers and that you will rely upon me wholly in that respect. Also she said she wanted the girls' mothers to write that they could go to New York, but I suppose that you will not have to say that as when I go to New York I go home.

I got a letter from Arthur Hyde telling me to be sure to come to West Point the last Saturday in October. Please can't you arrange to meet me at Garrison Saturday morning? I must go immediately.

Ever your loving daughter,
Fan

---

October 5

Dearest Mamsie,

My medicine powder all went to paste. I am taking it, paste or not, so please tell me what to do. Won't you send me a teaspoon, a napkin ring, a geometry compass, also a 12 inch ruler.

Tuesday night Florence and Isabelle McCurdy took several of us to Smith's for dinner. We had great fun and lots to eat, but missed our car coming home and took one chapel cut all around. We have only three a semester. Mr. Dean, the treasurer, died last night. We have only Thanksgiving day for a holiday and not the day after. Is that not *mean?* I would like to take Friday anyway or else get a doctor's excuse to stay home. I wish my pictures and pillows would get a gait on them, but don't bother yourself over them, as I can wait.

The Christians give the Freshmen a reception next Saturday night. I am going with Suzy Smith, a Senior and an old Brown girl. It will probably be horribly stupid. The Sophomores give the Freshmen a dance some time in November. I am going with a Miss Wendell. How I wish I had been able to go to dinner with you at the Astoria, Sunday night. Just think when you were ordering what you chose, your poor daughter was drinking coffee at a railroad station. Love, Love, Love. Tell Papa and Helen to write to their and your loving,

Fan

---

3 P.M. Friday afternoon, October seventh, 1898 A.D.

I thought I had better not come down this Saturday but wait until the next. Mrs. Kendrick says that half the Freshmen go on the 15th and half on the 22nd, so you see I can come to New York one of those dates and go to Mohonk the other. I just telegraphed you to send me a high-necked white organdie to wear at the Christians' reception Saturday (tomorrow), you see I tore my blue dress and my turquoise and white is too dressy. I don't know whether I can get it in time or not. I'm afraid you think I want things all the time. Can you send me a pincushion, a hand-glass (same shape as my silver one), and a china pen tray not longer than 9 inches? I suppose I could get most of these things in Poughkeepsie, but it is so hard to find time to go there.

I heard from Evelyn and Mary Banks today. Evelyn goes to Miss Ely's. There is to be a big ball in Scranton at New Years. Wouldn't it be fun to go? I must close now. Mrs. K.

never said boo about last Sunday. I don't believe she knew I went. Love to Daddy, the kid and yourself.

Lovingly,<br>Fan

---

October 8

Dearest Mamsie,

I have a very bad cold in my head, isn't that stupid of me? Oh! Mammie, it has been a horrid day. Raining all the time and so gloomy, and in neither mail today have I received a letter. Why did not some of you people write to me? I have not got a thing to tell you about. Oh dear, I must stop and do some Greek, it is so hard. How I do hate the place! Eleven weeks from yesterday Christmas vacation begins.

Your loving,<br>Fan

---

October 17

Dearest Papa,

I got your letter written from the Union League, last night. You must have had a grand old time at your dinner.

The one ambition of my life at present is to get to the Yale-Princeton game on the twelfth of November. I am afraid that Mrs. Kendrick won't let me go down on the 21st, go to West Point on the 29th, and then go down again on the 11th of November.

I have exactly ten dollars left but have kept pretty careful track of what I have spent. Books cost such a lot, and then it costs $3.00 to belong to Phil.

I know you hate long letters, so I shall stop.

Your loving daughter,<br>Fan

---

October 18

My dearest Mamsie,

Please do not put any more on my letters than Vassar

23

College, Poughkeepsie, New York. The building and room number are quite unnecessary and I don't like it. Don't let anyone else do it either.

Last night five Seniors came up to our room and we made them some chocolate and ate cookies, etc. Tell Auntie to have nice things specially for me to eat as I would certainly starve here if it weren't for Smiths and the cupboard in our room.

I have so much to do this week, I am about crazy, but of course do not worry the least bit. I never have worried over a lesson in my life.

Au revoir, ducky, love to everybody.

Your devoted,<br>Fan

---

October 25

My dear Mother,

Miss McCaleb, the secretary, sent for me the other day and asked me if I had ever had preparation at any other school than Miss Brown's, or if I had ever studied in the summer. I said no. She said the faculty were considering giving the certificate to Miss Brown's on account of my having passed my exams without condition.

Please have the waist of the skirt of my green dress made tight enough before you send it. Also the waist of the waist.

Your loving,<br>Fan

---

October 30

My dearest Mother,

I have simply not had a minute in which to write to you until now. Friday night was the children's party. That was great fun. There were so many funny costumes. And then Saturday we went to Lake Mohonk. I think there were about 250 girls. We went by trolley part of the way and then drove. When I saw the lake I certainly was astonished. It is nothing but a pond. *Half a mile* long and not very wide. The hotel is nice but the nicest thing about it is that there are innumerable pretty little walks and summer houses. Oh! dear if they would only fix green island at Lake George, they could make it a perfect paradise.

But as for Lake Mohonk being nicer than Lake George, it is not to my way of thinking. We had one accident coming home. One of the horses tried to run away and for some reason or another one of the girls jumped. She broke her ankle which has been broken before, and it is really quite serious. Her name is Lillian Bowen.

Please can you get me a programme of *The Adventures of Lady Ursula* and also of *The Christian*. Tell Papa not to forget the gum stickers.

About your coming up, do come next Saturday. I'm not yet unwell. Oh! Mammy, I do get so mad. Everything has seemed to go wrong since I left Lake George. I never had such a good time in my life as I had last summer. I didn't half realize what fun it was.

I'm glad you liked the violets. Did they look all right when they got there. Did he send 300?

It's about chapel time so I'm going to stop.

Lovingly,<br>Fan

---

November 1

Dearest Daddy,

Just about two seconds is mine before I go to English. Thank you lots and lots for the halloween pie. It was such a surprise. I never knew such people as you and Mother, always thinking of nice things.

I have just heard that the Sophomore party to the Freshmen is to be the 11th or 12th. I am *so* mad.

Lovingly,<br>Fan

Dearest Mamsie,

Birthday cake was good for halloween pie.

Tell Papa we must move down town before Christmas, that I don't want to come home for Christmas in Harlem. Either to the Fifth Avenue house* or any other nice house 60th to 80th streets, Fifth Avenue to Madison Avenue inclusive.

Why don't you bring some one with you on Saturday, an Aunt, a sister or some such creature. Only be sure to let me know beforehand, so I can get guest tickets for lunch.

I won't give up the ball game. I would like very much to have some nice man take me instead of Aunt Esther. Do you know of any and would you let me go with him if you did?

I feel *all* right, no headache or eye ache. The only trouble is my eyes are poor. They don't *see* well.

Lovingly,

Fan

*Mr. Simpson had bought a house at 988 Fifth Avenue. However, since his wife preferred living in Harlem at 11 Mt. Morris Park West, North West corner of 121st Street, at times the Fifth Avenue house was rented.*

---

My dear Kid Sister,

I am now at a Latin lecture but it is so stupid and boresome that instead of taking notes, I am going to try to keep awake by writing to you. (The Professor just tried to make a joke.) After the lecture I am going to take a walk and then I am going to get some ice cream and cake at Mrs. McGlyn's cottage. She is a nice funny Irish woman who keeps awfully good things to eat and sells them to the girls. Just think, I am coming home a week from tomorrow. Will you be glad to see me? Why does that stupid professor keep on talking? It is a beautiful day. I hope you are better, you foolish kid sister, the idea of your getting ill your first week at school. My! but I am glad that I can go to the Yale-Princeton game, though. If you ever happen to come across my old Yale flag, you must be sure to send it to me. You might also buy and send me some Yale ribbon, too, if you feel like going to 125th Street some day. Who is your *very* best fellow, now? Do persuade Papa to move down town before Christmas vacation, and *don't* let him forget to send me the gumstickers immediately. (Another joke by the Professor, te-he-te-he.) I shall be very mad if you don't pick up your feet and walk this way soon. You great old kid. I wonder what you're doing now. (Another attempt at a joke.) The Prof. is a handsome-looking man NIT. His clothes sort of hang on him and he talks along in the slowest stupidest way. One of his arms is akimbo (if you know what that means), and he stands nobly there before about 160 girls. Poor thing. Oh! he has stopped, it's all over so I must say goodbye.

Your loving sister,
Fan

---

November 15

My dear Daddy,

   Your two letters and the pictures arrived this morning but I have not yet received the seventy eight cents. Never mind about sending it, my accounts are all right, but is it not strange that it did not come? Please send the gum stickers.

Lovingly,
Fan

---

November 19

My dear Mother,

   Sue Smith, a Senior came up here today to see if I would have my name put up to serve on the committee for the second Hall Play. The first one is on the twenty-sixth of November. I believe it is quite an honor to serve.

27

Professor Van Ingen died last night, which is a terrible blow to the college. He had been here for 35 years. The gum stickers came this morning. Please thank Papa.

Most lovingly,
Fan

I am going to write to Ethel Boies and tell her I love her to distraction.

---

Dearest Mamsie,

Just got an invitation from George Baird for the Thanksgiving hop. Oh! Mother I am wild to go. Please won't you get Dad to write for rooms and meet me there. I can leave here on the 1.15 Wednesday, go to the hop that night, football game next morning and take the 12.40 for New York arriving at 125th street at 1.52 in time for dinner and the dentist afterwards. *Can't* you fix it. Other girls are coming home late so I can that night. Write me *immediately*.

Lovingly,
Fan

---

My dearest Mammy,

December 5

Really I have been so very busy Friday and Saturday that I did not have a minute to write. Friday noon after recitations Isabel and I went to Mrs. K. to see if we could take our men driving Saturday afternoon. She gave us permission if we could get a proper chaperone. So we ordered the rig and went to call on about every member of the faculty. All were either already taken, out, or had a previous engagement. That took a lot of time and then I had to write an essay to be ready by 6 P.M. We got our own supper in our rooms, dressed and were downstairs to receive our men at 7:30. Sterling came and he was perfectly great, brought me some American beauties, a box of Huylers and made himself otherwisely agreeable. I simply had the time of my life. Saturday morning we showed them around the grounds until the glee Club concert at 11 A.M. Some other girls, a Junior and two Sophomores asked us to join their driving party. So we did, Isabel, Florence Benedict and myself and our respective men. We had a great old time. The men left on the 6.25 and I was so dead tired I went to bed right after supper.

Yours lovingly,<br>Fanita

---

December 6

Dear Mammy   Mrs. K. won't let me come home until Christmas. She is certainly a pill. She refused lots of girls, saying it was too near vacation time. Must go to a recitation now. Goodbye, Fan

---

December 9

My dearest Mamsie,

I would like to have a luncheon for some of the Brown girls, but I am afraid we will have to arrange the details when I get home (two weeks from today at 1.30). As for Christmas shopping, I don't know what to say, of course I want Christmas presents for people but I don't know what I want. I like gym very much now, but I think it will get monotonous. I'll bring the Miscellany home Christmas. There is nothing of mine in it, and probably never will be. But there are some pretty good things in it just the same. At last I am unwell, yesterday the eighth.

Thank the kid for her letter, and tell her I may write to her.

Lovingly,<br>Fan

My dear Fanny,

I really don't know how to write to you, so I will try different styles. How is this?

Dear Miss Simpson,

I wish to inform you I arrived safely. I trust you will pass a pleasant year.

Yours sincerely,
Sterling Beardsley.

No, that won't do at all, it is too formal, and you might judge from that that I didn't care for you. How is this?

Dear Fanny,

I arrived safely after a very comfortable trip. I left on the midnight train Sunday night which was a few minutes late in starting. I found everybody well here. I even found the ink well. I arose this morning at 8 o'clock and went to breakfast . . . and so on.

Sincerely,
Sterling.

Now I think that is pretty good. There is nothing in it which you could say was insincere or a jolly. It is very practical, the only fault being that it is egoistic. Still it is pretty good. Now maybe you like this.

My own precious little girl,

You don't know with what mingled pain and sorrow I took leave of you on Sunday. It seemed as if the whole world was . . . etc.*****

Always your devoted,
Sterling.

Do you like that? True it is a little ultra, Fanny, but I don't doubt that many such letters are written. I could still have another style and it would go something like this.

30

Dearest Fanny, (or Fan)

You certainly are the dearest girl alive. You don't know what pleasure you gave me while at Poughkeepsie . . . etc.

Lovingly,

Sterling.

Now that is not so bad is it? It is not so ultra as the one preceding and you may like it.

Oh Fanny, I don't know how to write to you, you see. Let me know if you like any of the above forms of styles and I will surely adopt it, (to you).

I write just as I feel and I hope to write natural. I never stop to think what to write, but I just go on like Tennyson's brook, and only stop when I come to, and think how I am afflicting myself on the reader. Then I stop and am called a jollier for writing as I feel. Moral: never be natural but write according to Ruth Ashmore.

Next time you write I will study your letter, begin one the same way, use same wording only different thought and idea, and end it the same way. Then maybe you can say, "Well Sterling is sincere, and writes an interesting letter."

Well don't forget me, Fanny, I am going to say 'Au revoir' now. With kindest regards, I am as ever,

Faithfully,

Sterling.

---

December 12

My dear Mamsie,

Thank you ever so much for the box, which has not yet come. I wish you would not send anything Saturday morning hereafter, I have been having more trouble about it. The dress arrived and I like it very much. It fits well except to be taken up on the shoulders in the back. I don't know how they are going to do it, as the back and collar are all in one piece. The skirt trains a little in the back and just touches right in the middle of the front but is all right on the sides. I don't believe

31

the front needs to be touched, however, as when I stand up straight it is all right. The size around the waist is fine. I wonder how it happened so. Please, can't you get my presents for Papa and the kid. Also some little things for the two McCurdys, Florence B. and Mary M.

Are you going to make dress-maker's appointments, shampoos etc. for Friday afternoon.

Tell Dr. Secord that there is no use in sending my tooth powder *now*. He might as well keep it and give it to me for Christmas.

The box has just come and Florence has gone down to get it delivered up here.

Good-bye, Mamma.

Lovingly,<br>Fan

---

December 13

My dear Mammy,

Having just a minute, I am going to write a wee note to you.

Mary did not tell me where they were going to stay in New York. She just said at the same hotel where Ruby Newcomb is.

The express company here is simply fool. You must never believe a thing they say.

I guess the Van Nests are quite swell in New York society, but I don't like Miss Van Nest's chin, do you?

I must stop. Ever your loving,

Fan

---

December 14

My dear Daddy,

I really don't know what I want for Christmas. You and Mama, I know, want to give me some *grand* thing. I would like to move down town for a Christmas present.

There is only one express a day and that gets out to the college at three o'clock. When a package misses that you have to pay 40 cents to have it brought out.

As for my calling cards, please find out from Dempsey and Carroll exactly what is the latest thing and most proper. (I would like to have 988 Fifth Avenue down in the corner).

Do write me a longer letter and tell me that you will be tickled to death to see me on the twenty third.

Tell Mama I am afraid she will have to get all of my Christmas presents to give away. I am in the midst of exams.

Lovingly,<br>
Fan

---

December 28<br>
Scranton, Pa.

My dearest Mother,

Had a very short pleasant trip. Train was on time. Ethel Boies, Dave and two men who are staying here, met me with a closed conveyance.

I feel perfectly and am perfectly all right, so don't worry a bit. Went driving this afternoon. Bundled up warmly.

Must get dressed.

Lovingly,<br>
Fan

---

January 10, 1899

My dear Mammy,

There were lots of girls on the train I knew and I got a seat near them. Florence was here and I went to bed.

Lovingly,<br>
Fan

---

January 12

You dear little Mammy, the idea of your taking my foolish

words seriously. Now really I shall not like it at all if you don't write me lots of nice letters as you used to.

Everything is just exactly the same and I almost feel as if I had never been away for vacation. Isa is homesick as usual. Janet hates to study, so did not return. Talk about good times, well none of them are in it with the one I had. It was just bully.

People are beginning to talk about semester exams already, but you know I never did worry much over exams.

I am planning now to come home on the third of February. What do you think about my bringing Mary Marshall down then? I don't believe Mrs. K. would hear of my going to West Point on the fourteenth. However, I am going to try to work it somehow.

Lovingly yours,<br>Fan

---

January 13

My dear Papa,

Please send me the newspaper which contained Colonel Waring's report of the condition of Havana. I think it was in either last Sunday's or Monday's paper. I have to write an abstract on it for Hygiene. Dr. Thelberg called on me first today to stand up and read my paper on plumbing, which I proceeded to do. She said it was very good and that the plumbing of the house was perfect. (Are you not glad?)

I have just been putting a new blotter on my desk. Will you please send me a lot of rubber ends, no pencils though.

Well, good-night, love and kisses to Mama and the kid.

Your devoted daughter,<br>Fan

---

January 24

My dear little Mammy,

A great big white ulcer formed on my gum again today,

but it has not ached and I jabbed it with a needle so I guess it will be all right.

I got my permission for February third today. Nobody has found out about last Saturday. I certainly think it will be nice to go to the Philharmonic on the third. Mary Marshall is ill now (I think it is malaria), but I guess she will be well next week. If she is not, I will bring someone else. Perhaps a McCurdy.

Have you decided about moving yet? Be sure to let me know when you do. Must go to Greek.

Lovingly,
Fan

---

January 30

My dear Mother,

I have just a wee bit of time before the mail goes. Here is my exam schedule:

Monday — Math at 10.50
Tuesday — Latin at 10.50
Wednesday — English at 8.20
Thursday — Greek at 10.50
Friday — Hygiene at 8.20

Now I must go over and study a skeleton and a heart so au revoir.

Lovingly,
Fan

---

February 6

Dear Mammy,

When the train got to Fishkill, who should get on but Florence Benedict. We came up together and I found no flunk notes on my arrival. Mary stayed all night with me, and as she has a headache, she is not going to get up yet.

Lovingly,
Fan

Dear little Mammy,

Mrs. K. gave me permission to go to the Point on the fourteenth. Isn't she bully?

Mary is in the infirmary. I am afraid that she is quite ill. The grippe has attacked her again and the doctor is afraid of bronchitis. Poor dear, she is worried about missing her lessons.

Oh! you silly little goose, to think anything about what I said on Saturday. I just thought it might not be as nice for Mary.

Please I want my pink and yellow dress, my gray cape, long gloves, etc.

Lovingly,
Fan

---

February 9

My dear Mother,

I guess you had better take a small trunk to the Point. Don't forget my nightgown and other necessaries including a curling iron. Also my new black satin slippers and some stockings. And please Mother, could you get me some feather arrangement for my hair. I think yellow would go better than pink.

Mary is about the same. She suffers with the back of her head a great deal. I don't see why the doctors don't stop that, I should think they could.

Please I want to be sure to leave here on the 1.15 as there may be something (as cavalry drill), going on Tuesday afternoon.

My dear, Mrs. Kendrick was as docile as a lamb, I never was so surprised.

Ever your most devoted,
Fan

Dearest Mother,

Now my plan is this: you arrive at Cranston's at 1.05, go to the hotel, get your dinner and then go to Craney's. I arrive at Garrison's at 1.59, at Craney's about 2.20 and meet you there. Then we see about getting a room (and on account of the storm, we may be able to get one) and I see my cadets.

So au revoir until 2.20 tomorrow.

Lovingly,<br>Fan

---

February 15

My dear Mother,

Please don't think anything more about that trip to West Point. I will go some other time (if the fates are not against it). Of course I was furiously disappointed, but I will get over it. No mails have come from New York today, due to the storm. I just wrote George Baird explaining.

Everybody has been making and receiving valentines. All the Senior tables were decorated with hearts tonight and the room looked very pretty.

The doctor says that Mary is some better. I think it would be very nice, if you should send her some flowers now.

I must stop and study.

Lovingly,<br>Fan

---

February 17

My dear Mother,

I got the finest valentine from Miss Stevens (she is the teacher who sits at our table you know). I got a dandy note and my hop card from George Baird. He said there was a proverb that the third time never fails and he'd tried Thanksgiving and Graduation, so wouldn't I please give him Easter. And Oh! Mama, just think Charlie Romeyn, the great football man was on it. Two girls from here went to the hop. They walked across the river and had a gorgeous time.

And Oh! Mama, just guess what. Don't breathe it to anyone, but Mr. and Mrs. McCurdy are coming on and they are going to take Isabel away with them. You know she does not like it here. Flicker (Florence McCurdy) is going to stay here. Isabel is not going home and she is talking about going to Miss Brown's. You see Bess Hine is there, and Isa would not have to study very hard.

It is time to mail this, so au revoir.

Lovingly,

Fan

---

February 18

My dear Mammy,

Just guess what. Mr. Marshall arrived yesterday and is determined to take Mary back with him. He says that if he doesn't do that Mrs. Marshall will come on here and as she has been ill for two years and is very nervous and an invalid, it would probably do her a great deal of harm. Dr. Thelberg saw Isabel and asked her to talk to Mr. Marshall and try to persuade him not to move Mary. Dr. Thelberg said that Mary was warding off typhoid, and that if Mr. Marshall moved her, it would be taking her life in his hands. Mr. and Mrs. McCurdy arrive this morning so perhaps they will be able to influence him. Dr. Thelberg even sent Isabel to talk to Mary and try to influence *her*. Florence McCurdy does not know what she is going to do for a room-mate when her sister leaves. I should like to room with her but of course I won't leave Florence B. Everything is so mixed up. The doctor thinks Mary's New York trip finished her up. Poor child!

Lovingly yours,

Fan

Dear little Mother,

Mr. McCurdy talked to Mr. Marshall yesterday and I think he about persuaded him to leave Mary here. The flowers arrived all right and were lovely. I am going in town with the McCurdys today. They have not yet decided what to do.

On Washington's birthday, which is Wednesday, everybody has to dress up as George or Martha Washington. They want me to dress as George. I have not a thing to wear. Could you not go to a costumers and get me a George Washington suit, I suppose I would need a wig too. If you can't get a man's get a Martha Washington costume. You would have to send it Tuesday at the *very latest*. Please try, Mammy, as I have not a thing to wear.

The tables are going to be decorated and the girls are going to wear their costumes to dinner, the George Washingtons wearing skirts over their trousers. Then in the evening we have a ball in Phil. Hall (the men dropping their skirts). Of course I would have to have very full trousers, or Mrs. K. would not approve.

Don't you think it is mean that they don't give us a holiday on Washington's birthday?

The box last week arrived on the three o'clock express. (I am not unwell yet.) Please don't be melancholy about my not getting to the Point. It isn't as though that's the only chance I'll ever have. I'm going Easter if I can.

Please send me some sort of a costume. You are evidently not going to move. Has Daddy rented the Fifth Avenue house for longer? Oh dear, I suppose he has.

Lovingly,
Fan

---

February 25

My dear Mother,

Mr. Marshall went home a few days ago and we saw Dr.

Thelberg last night. She said that Mary was *alarmingly worse,* that her fever had gone up to 106 and that she considered it very serious and had telegraphed Mr. Marshall. Isn't that awful! I have not seen the doctor this morning, but I am going to try to do so.

I want to get this in the mail.

Lovingly,
Fan

---

February 27

My dear Mother,

Yesterday morning the doctor got a telegram from Mr. Marshall asking whether he should bring Mrs. Marshall with him. The doctor telegraphed back yes, so this afternoon they both arrived. Today I have been hearing first that she is worse, then that she is better, and I really don't know what to believe. I think the Doctor was quite relieved when the Marshalls came. Oh! I wish Mary would get better. I think they are afraid that the rheumatism will settle around her heart.

The McCurdys get back from New York tonight.

Lovingly,
Fan

---

February 28

My dear Mother,

Mary is no better, no worse (I'm afraid though, that if she does not soon begin to get better, it means she is worse). The Doctor told Isabel that Sunday morning she did not expect Mary to live four hours. Her mother and father don't think she is as ill as she really is, because they found her alive when they got here.

How is the kid? I hope better.

Lovingly,
Fan

Dearest Mammy,

Mary is still critically ill, but slightly better. Her mother is the funniest thing, she does not seem to think it serious at all and today she did not come out to college from town until the afternoon. Please I want some money, tell Papa. Please I want a tailor made spring suit made at a very swell tailor down town. Tell Daddy I want it muchly. Must go to bed.

Lovingly,<br>Fan

---

March 3

Dearest Mammy,

The doctor from Poughkeepsie came out again to see Mary. He said that though not yet *out of danger,* she was very much better than last week.

Please did you send me my dress? It is for Helen Crosby in the Hall Play. You see, I take it over to the hall and put it on her myself. When she comes off the stage, I take it off her myself and take it home. I will be very careful of it, dear.

Chapel bell just rang.

Lovingly,<br>Fan

---

March 7

My dearest Mammy,

Regular blizzard. Snowing like thunder.

I did not ask anybody for next Friday, and would be delighted to go in General Andrew's box.

I am glad Helen is better. I think it would do her lots of good to go to Atlantic City. I wish I had time to go. Give the kid my love. Don't you think this is a grand idea? Next week you take the kid to Atlantic City and stay with her there 'til the 27th. On the 24th I arrive and get just the few days rest and sea-air I need. I am so tired, I must go to bed, dear.

Lovingly,
Fan

---

March 14

Well, Mammy dear, we are all about wild up here. Grace Hecker hit her head today and about an hour afterward became unconscious and was taken to the infirmary. That was at 6.30. At eight o'clock she had not regained consciousness. Mary Marshall is very low. On Friday night she had a chill and her temperature went from 95 to 105. On Saturday night she had another chill. Sunday night her temperature went down, but she did not have a chill. Grace Bruce is in the infirmary with pleurisy, and Florence McCurdy is in there with the backache. Another girl is quarantined with chicken pox, and Agnes Slosson (a freshman I know), is at a hospital in Poughkeepsie having an operation on her ear. Dr. Taylor prayed for Mary on Saturday.

Your daughter is all right, but must stop and go to bed. Have you decided about Atlantic City yet?

Lovingly,
Fan

---

Wednesday, A.M. For Mammy alone.

My dear Mother,

Mary is about the same. Am awfully glad you have written for rooms at Atlantic City. At last, Mammy dear, I am unwell. Night before last.

The dress suitcase came all right. Thank you.

Lovingly,
Fan

42

Dearest Mammy,

Have not had a minute to write. Mary has had a comfortable time since I last wrote. Grace is better, and going home tomorrow. Her sister (who married the Hungarian) came yesterday and will take her home. The afternoon Grace was hurt, she was playing in a basketball game with the Juniors. They were playing in the gym and Grace was running. Before she could stop herself she struck the wall with her head, and the girls behind her knocked against her. She got up and went on playing. Shortly after the game ended and she went home to Strong she became unconscious. They have forbidden us to play basketball in the gym any more. Flicker (Florence, to you) McCurdy went home today. Please send Mary some gorgeous flowers.

Lovingly,<br>Fan

---

Mother dearest,

Thank you ever and ever so much for the box. It was well packed and everything arrived in good condition.

The last Hall Play of the year took place last night. It was *The Private Secretary*. Though good, it was not as good as the last one, *Christopher Jr.* Julia Stimson was a man in the play last night. She made a dandy looking man, but did not act very well.

Thank you so much for the sample of the piqué dress, which you did *not* enclose.

I have got my ticket, trunk check etc. but have not yet begun to pack. I am coming home on the 12 o'clock train. Love to Papa and the kid.   Most lovingly,   Fan

P.S.   Tell the kid RUBBER. If you go to Atlantic City on Thursday, and I come home on Friday, how am I going to manage about packing my trunk for Atlantic City? Don't forget to write me whether I am to go to 42nd Street, then to Altman's and then to the dentist, or get off at Harlem and go to the dentist and then to Altman's. I would love to *have some girl* at Atlantic City with me if you and Papa thought best, either Mary Banks or Daisy Hanes. Please if you do think best, ask the girl yourself immediately. Isabel McCurdy wants to go home New York way, but her ferry for her train leaves at 7.25 P.M. Friday night, and she would be alone in the city during the afternoon, and would have to escort herself to the station, so she is going to go home the other way. If you and Helen go to Atlantic City on Thursday, please ask Frances Warren to spend the night with me.   F.

---

April 7

Dearest Mother,

Mrs. K., after some hesitation, gave me my permission, so I will see you at the Point. The McCurdys are not yet back, and I've heard nothing from them. Their Grandmother must be worse.

I do hope your cold is better, dear, take good care of yourself. I think all the jewelry I want is my little diamond breast pin — the bow knot effect. I don't want my bell-button chain.

Lovingly,
Fan

---

April 13

Oh! Mother, Hurrah! At four o'clock this afternoon I saw Mary. She was very bright and cheerful, quite like her natural self. I talked to her for ten minutes. I was her first visitor for a month. She sent lots of love and thanks to you and said that she would write you as soon as she could. This morning she sat up in a rocking chair and for breakfast she had some oysters, so you see she is much better.

Got a new way of fixing my hair à la M. de C.B. Must stop and retire to my downy cot.

Lovingly,<br>Fan

---

April 17

Dearest Mother,

Thank you ever so much for the fine box of food.

Do you know that I had a physical exam, and I have gained five pounds since the fall. That is perfectly accurate as I was weighed on the same scales, both times clothed in merely a smile.

Mammy, I don't know what to do about getting home. If I ask Mrs. K. about getting permission, I *know* she won't let me go both times; so I think that next week I shall take a French leave, and the week after that ask for permission.

Tell Papa that he is the greatest man I know. The idea of having that kodak picture enlarged! It was very good of Abby, but vile of me. It arrived safely, but I won't have it hung up in my room.

How is little Mammy and her cold? I hope they have separated.

Lovingly,<br>Fan

---

April 14

Dearest Mother,

Thank you for sending me *Aftermath.*

Mary is still improving and Isabel is getting better. She has to have her ears treated four times a day. For the last few days nobody but room-mates of patients have been allowed in the Infirmary, but I have worked Mother Flett to let me in. Visitors hours are from 12-1 and 5-6, but sometimes Mother Flett lets me in other times, and last night I took dinner in there with Isabel. This is a very great honor, and Mother Flett

45

always impresses it on one what a very great favor she is doing.

I have so many plans and so little time. I want to bring Isabel down with me Founders. Sometime I want to have Eleanor Samson, sometime Florence Benedict, sometime I want to visit in Albany, sometime I want to go to West Point; there are lots of people I want to have here to spend Saturday with me. Field Day is some Saturday the first part of May, and I guess there are match basketball games every Saturday in May. Please will you tell me how I am going to do all those things and keep in my right mind?!

Ever your loving,
Fan

After my luncheon at Sherry's at two o'clock, I must return on the 7.30 train. (I myself think Mrs. K. is somewhat of a pig)

---

April 19

Dearest Mother,

I was very much surprised to get your letter saying that you had written to Mrs. K. I was rather sorry that you wrote, but perhaps it is just as well. Now Mammy, about our plans. First for this week. Friday at 3.20 I will be at 138th street. I suppose that you have some dress-makers appointments for me. Just now Florence B. is in the infirmary with cramps, but she is coming out tomorrow and will be all right by Friday. Shall I bring her down?

Now about the April 27-30 trip. I am quite sure Mrs. K. will let the McCurdys come. I want a theatre party either Thursday or Saturday night. I would like to have Theo Mc-Graw (Please write him yourself immediately), Sterling Beardsley (his address is 170 Ocean Avenue, Brooklyn or else telephone) and some other men, Fred Reynolds, Harry Fisher or any old body.

Now about plays. The McCurdys have seen *The Great Ruby*, O'Neill in *The Musketeers*, but have not seen *Rupert of*

46

*Hentzau, Lord and Lady Algy.* I want the McCurdy's theatre party the grandest out.

Yesterday afternoon I went out and played basketball, I madly adore it. I am so stiff that I can hardly wiggle my legs.
Lovingly,<br>Fan

---

May 2

Dearest Mother,

Well, of all unlucky girls, your daughter is the worst. She drew 109th choice for a room and got a parlor with three bed-rooms in Main with Caroline Stoddard and Ruth Johnson. The girls are fine but the room —

Please write and tell me that I need not come back if I don't want to.

Must stop. Will be home for good (Thank the good Lord) five weeks from next Thursday.
Lovingly,<br>Fan

---

May 3

Dearest Mammy,

Please don't worry at all about my room as I very likely may be able to make some exchange next fall.

And anyway the bedrooms are not so bad. It is on the fourth floor where there is lots of air and Caroline and Ruth are *dandy* girls. It is in the south wing facing south. It is a parlor with three bedrooms (Two of them corridor), you live in each bedroom one third of the year. I have quit thinking about rooms entirely. Florence Benedict drew 4th choice in singles — about the best thing she could have drawn.

What about you and Aunt Esther coming up for Field Day next Saturday. I would love to have Arthur come up here some time in the Spring, but I don't believe he would enjoy

47

it much next Saturday, as of course he could not see the Field Day exercises or the basketball game.

For goodness sake, send me some low shoes of some kind. I have to wear *high* lace boots with my short skirt.

Lovingly,
Fan

---

May 8

Dearest Mammy,

First match game of basketball yesterday. We beat the sophomores 4 to 0. Hurrah for 1902! Tickled, well I just rather guess!

The other day we went down the river a little further than Newburgh. It was lots of fun.

Most dinner time, so will stop.

Lovingly,
Fan

---

May 15

Dearest Mother,

Hurrah for us! 1900 and 1902 beat 1901 and '99 by the score of 4 to 2. It was simply great. No one was hurt, and everyone played splendidly. Hurrah for 1902! We are *the Class ! ! !*

Three weeks from next Thursday.

Lovingly,
Fan

---

May 25

Dearest Mammy,

Yesterday Papa sent me a sample of wall paper from Lake George. I am not sure whether I like it or not. I rather wish he had not gone ahead and put in tile without consulting me. I would like to plan my room myself. I got the samples from you today. I think I like the striped with the wreaths best and the striped one with the dot effects second best. Please tell me *absolutely frankly, your unbiased opinion,* which you like best. I am going to look at them again in the morning and see which is the better blue. Would *you* like plain paper better? I have always found that in the end I have liked what you picked out better than what I picked out, so please aid me. As to the beds, I want twin beds, either plain brass or white with lots of brass trimmings. Perhaps the latter would go better with the room. Whatever *you* say. As to the carpet, I think I want matting.

Good night Duckie,

Lovingly,
Fan

---

May 26

Dearest Mammy,

It is almost time to hand in our elections for next year, so I thought I'd write and tell you about it. The required work is as follows: English — 3 hours, History — 3 hours, and either Chemistry or Physics — 3 hours. Then we have 6 hours elective. The following are the subjects I *can* elect for the first semester: Latin, Greek, Math., Geology, Descriptive Astronomy, French, German, Old English, 3 hours each. Of course I shall have to go a good deal by the schedule so as not to have any conflicts, and not to have any recitation the first two hours Monday morning, or late Friday afternoon. I think it rests between Greek, Latin, Geology (a snap) and Astronomy. Sent the wall-paper samples back. Want either striped paper or plain.

Most lovingly,
Fan

---

May 28

It is Sunday afternoon and I (with two other girls), am lying on some pillows in the grass on top of Sunset Hill. It is fine and shady and there is a beautiful breeze, so while you are probably sizzling in New York, I am cool and comfortable. Just think, a week from next Thursday I shall be home for good. I think I shall elect Greek and Astronomy next year. No matter how I fix it, I shall have to have a recitation on Friday afternoon from 2.45 to 3.45. Please, Mammy, tell Papa I want some money (about $15.) very much. I have some bills to pay, class picture, express bill, freight bill, food etc. I have arranged to have a man down town pack my pictures, pillows and bagdad and send them by freight to Lake George. I am going to leave my china and tea-kettle here, also my furniture and curtains. My capsules arrived all right and I have taken them somewhat regularly. My chin is all right. I would like to have a bathing suit made just as I want it for next summer. Do you think I can have it done? Is Feinberg making you a yachting suit? Don't forget to tell him about the two white collars for my gray suit. I do hope it will fit right. The big June hop is on the ninth. Please ask Papa to telegraph for a room. I would like to go up just for that night anyway. How do you think it would be for me to ask Helen Crosby to go to the Point with me that night. I think I could get someone to make out her card. However, it might be too much trouble. Just as you say about it. Please send the money as soon as possible. My exams finish at 10.20 Thursday June 8th. Of course I shall come home by first train I can get, but don't dare say when anymore.

Lovingly,<br>Fan

---

May 30<br>Purity and Wisdom — A.D. 1861

Dearest little Mother,

The Senior Howl takes place today. They have been off on the river all afternoon and tonight have a big dinner in the gym. It is the first day of Senior vacation. (How I do envy those Seniors). I am perfectly crazy to get to a place where I can eat and sleep all I want to. Florence and I got desperate this afternoon so we went to Smiths to dinner. There was a parade in town (quite exciting), but we did not get any holiday at all at all.

Please don't say that you did not like the tone of my letter to Helen. Of course I shall try to pass but the exams are going to be hard and you must not be surprised if I flunk any.

Got a letter from Isabel yesterday and one from Flicker today. They are having a fine time keeping house. They have seen Mary Marshall once and she is better though improving slowly. She can get dressed but cannot walk alone yet. Her hair has come out somewhat, but it is also coming in. She talks of coming back continually, and fully expects to. Dr. Thelberg and Miss McCaleb say not until February. Thank you very much for the money.

Love to Papa from whom I got a letter from the lake, and the kid from whom I want a letter, and yourself.

Lovingly,
Fan

---

June 1

Dearest Mother,

Hot! It is simply unbearable. If it is this way next week, I think there will be a sorry lot of exam papers.

We just had a class meeting. Caroline Sperry and Frances Fenton were put up for president for next year. Caroline got it, for which I am very sorry, as I wanted Frances. I have decided to take Greek and Astronomy next year. (Did I tell you?) I will have a recitation on Friday afternoon, which jars me quite considerably, but no class on Monday morning until 11.20.

Must stop and study.

Lovingly,
Fan

June 3rd

Dearest Mother,

Please send me at once six of my photographs. I have promised some of the girls to send for them. Oh! I have so much to do: review Latin, pack, attend the Senior auction, attend Basketball game for championship between '99 and 1900 etc. We had a math written lesson yesterday which was rather a terror.

Lovingly,
Fan

---

June 4th, Sunday afternoon

Dearest Mother,

You just ought to see this room! The pictures are down and together with my pillows and bagdad, golf clubs and tea kettle, shipped to Lake George. Everything is topsy turvy. I have a box and some excelsior in which I am packing the things I am going to leave here. Between times I have been cramming for my Latin, which is going to be a holy terror, *but* I am going home Thursday. I have my trunk check (to 125th St.) and my ticket. Last night there was the best show given by '99 in Phil. Hall. First there was a minstrel show. The girls had blacked up (half men and half girls). The songs and jokes were simply *great*. Theo's friend, Liz Jenkins, was quite the star of the occasion. Then there was a faculty meeting. The girls made up to look just like the professors, and imitated them to perfection. Then refreshments.

I suppose when you get this the kid will be on her way to Lake George.

Lovingly,
Fan

---

June 6

Dearest Mother,

Well two exams are over, Latin and English, much to my delight. I do hope I got through all right and I really have hopes that I did. You never can tell though. Dutton (in Latin) flunks anybody she happens to think of. If it were only not so hot! It is really almost unbearable. This room is just under the roof and has sun all day long. In today's exam, Dr. Thelberg came in and told us to take off our collars, and they had ice water supplied over there.

I forgot to thank you for the box. It was perfectly fine, and certainly the salvation of the North Tower.

Of all things, Mammy, I must have a bathing suit and some thin white dresses. I hate to think of shopping this hot weather. We'll do things just as quickly as possible and get away to the lake, won't we?

Please excuse paper and pencil but I have used up all except my class paper, which is packed, and have washed out my ink-well, and put it away for next year.

Most lovingly,
Fan

## SOPHOMORE YEAR

September 23, 1899

My dearest Mother,

Well the train got to Poughkeepsie at 4.40 and out I got. The doctor got out too. He is the fussiest man I ever saw. Just before we got to the station he again told me that sometimes on the cars he felt so nauseated that he had to recline all the time.

When I got to the college I found that Cecil Nield was not coming back. When I went up for the key to my room, Miss Cornwall said Mrs. Kendrick wanted to see me. I asked Mrs. K. if I could have G. Hecker for my room-mate. She positively refused as there is a rule that no sophomore with a certain amount of conditions can room in Strong. I asked for Ruth Johnson, Maude Wright and none of them could. I was in despair. Finally I told her that Maude had an exam this morning, which might pass off her condition. After a lot of red tape, she finally put Maude over here. So here I am in 28 Strong with Maude Wright. She is not the girl I would have chosen, but I suppose I am fortunate to get anybody, and she really is very nice.

Must stop now and go see if my trunk has come.

Lovingly,
Fan

P.S. I dressed in 20 minutes this morning!

---

September 24

Dearest Mother,

Have just begun to unpack my trunk. We shall need two curtains, one for each door between the study and bedrooms. Striped silk. Also two white curtains for the windows in our study. For goodness sake express me the trunk from Lake George with about seven pillows, the hard green cushion, my bagdad and the pictures I picked out. Ask Papa to see that there is a wire on each picture frame.

Also a piece of Ivory soap, Pear's soap, some dusters and a pen knife. You will be glad to know that I have a very large closet, and that there is a bathroom with nice tubs next door. Also I want two matchsafes like the kind I described, and a chafing dish.

Dear little Mammy, have you missed me? Well I have missed you too. I am just settling down, but it *is* rather hopeless to think I have the whole long winter before me. I wish winter was four months long and summer eight. I am afraid I am a lazy duffer. Love to all my relatives and friends at the Lake.

Fan

---

September 26

My dearest Mother,

Prexy announced in chapel tonight that there would be a holiday on Friday, Dewey Day. So that I have absolutely nothing to do from 12:20 on Thursday until 11:20 on Monday. I don't want to stay in Poughkeepsie and I am crazy to be in New York. I would give absolutely everything I possessed if you and Daddy were going to be in New York. Ed Clark and Frank Fuller have written and asked if I was going to be in N.Y. this week, as they are both going to be there.

Now, Mother, I don't want to loaf here those few days. Prexy said that we need not even ask permission to go away, we just have to register.

I tell you what I would like to do if possible. I would like to go to New York and visit Frances Warren. You see she is my best friend, and it would be my last chance before she is married. So I shall telegraph her tomorrow, and ask whether she can have me. And then I shall await your decision. We could have lots of fun, ask Ed and Frank to come see us Thursday and have grand fun. I don't care so much about seeing the Dewey celebrations, but I would like to get away when I have vacation.

Now, Mammy, I will telegraph Frances. And you must telegraph *immediately* what you think I had better do. Goodbye, Mammy dear.

Lovingly,
Fan

*Darn* Prexy. Why does he not warn us some weeks ahead when he is going to give us a holiday.

---

*The following note was left at the Waldorf-Astoria, to be delivered by hand. Mr. and Mrs. Simpson always spent a few days at a hotel in New York, between their summer at Lake George and their winter months at 11 Mt. Morris Park West. Presumably this was to give the servants some vacation as well as time to clean the house.*

September 30

My dearest Mammy,

The unexpected always happened, I mean happens. And

Oh! my dear, you are just too sweet to have let me come to visit Frances. I have had *the* time of my life. Frank is staying at the Waldorf, and Frances, Allan and I will come down some time Sunday afternoon. Probably about half past three. As Frank has a room on the 3rd floor, Fifth Avenue side, we went down there to lunch today and watched the parade from his window. I go back on Monday morning.

Love to Daddy and the kid. Mostly your mostest lovingest sweetheart daughter.

Fanita

---

October 2

My dear Mother,

Well my holiday is past and gone. Oh! it was such fun. The best time I ever had. Talk about seeing the parade! Did I not strike a cinch?! Well, I just guess I did see it!

Say Mother, don't read this out loud, but please buy and send me some drawers P.D.Q. I have not any clean ones left.

On the 16th there is to be a wedding rehearsal in the evening. Perhaps I had better try to get away from Friday until Wednesday the week of the wedding. Please have my bridesmaid's dress the prettiest thing that ever happened.

Lovingly,<br>Fan

---

October 10

My dearest Mother,

Yesterday I went to Mrs. K. and she was quite docile. She gave me leave of absence for the wedding from Tuesday until Thursday. So you can expect me home on the 1.15 Tuesday the 17th, arriving at the 138th St. Station at 3.19. Then I think I had better go home, change my corsets and go to Miss Tucker's for a final trying on of my bridesmaid's gown.

Now Mammy dear, please don't worry the least bit about Frank Fuller and myself. *It is all right.* We are just good friends, and you know that I would not think of anything else while I am in college. As for being on my guard, why Mammy, all the men I know think I am a perfect iceberg.

Maul that kid sister of mine for me, will you? And tell her that she is getting entirely too frisky, skipping a class, the freak.

Love to you and Daddy on your wedding day the ninth.

Most devotedly,
Fan

---

October 14

Dearest Mother,

Have been busy all morning mending clothes, sewing shields, putting up pictures. Tonight Maude and I are going to have a party. Our room is about finished and we have a box of food. Twelve guests are invited and the invitations read as follows: "Mr. and Mrs. Simpson request the pleasure of Miss . . . . . .'s company at the opening of their new home, Villa Bohemia, on Saturday evening October fourteenth at eight o'clock. N.B. Guests are requested to eat a very light dinner." Thank you for the box of lovely food.

Yesterday morning I made oxygen for two hours and then washed dishes. Our team won yesterday in basketball. We made two goals and the other side none. *I* made one of the goals. Am not one bit stiff.

Lovingly,
Fanita

---

October 22

The play last night, *A Rice Pudding*, was good. This morning the Bishop of Wilmington, Delaware preached. He is a nice old man, but preached a *long* sermon. With great haste.

Lovingly,
Fan

October 28

My dearest Mother,

Thank you for the box of food. The stocks, petticoat and pictures also came. Tell Papa thank you for the pictures. Also tell him that I get *Life* regularly. I am afraid the petticoat will have to be altered as I cannot pull up the drawstring around my waist (because the drawstring does not extend all the way around).

I shall have to take my plaid flannel waist back to Altman's and see if they will give me a new one. The back has fallen to pieces in the most remarkable way.

The Seniors gave us a Halloween party last night. Must stop.

Lovingly,<br>
Fan

P.S.   Many Happy returns of yesterday, your birthday. We do not know here whether we are going to have Thanksgiving vacation on the 23rd or the 30th. The catalogue says the 23rd, and Pres. McKinley the 30th. If we have it the 30th, we shall probably have both Thursday and Friday vacation. Then I shall come to New York, and would like to have the McCurdys visit me. I do miss them at college. We could have lots of fun. Get up some sort of a spree and have Sterling, Frank, Fred, and Theo and *perhaps* Helen Halsey.

---

November 2

My dear little Mother,

What under the sun is the matter with you? Of course I read your letters, wouldn't do without them for anything. I always have time to read letters, though I have very little time to write them.

Mother mine, I really believe that you are homesick. Now *that* won't do, at all, at all. Just think of all the girls here whose families don't see them from September until December and again from December until June. We are very lucky to have college so near New York. If you want to come up the middle of the week, Thursday afternoon is the best for me.

Now Maude and I are going for a long walk and then I am coming in to study. Am still *well*, I can't imagine what is the matter.

Devotedly,<br>Fanita

---

November 3

Dearest Mother,

I think I shall follow your advice and wear my rosebud silk to the Senior Parlor Opening. It would probably be the better plan. Have Argumentation to prepare for next hour, so farewell.

Lovingly yours,<br>Fanita

---

November 6

My dear Mother,

A freshman, named Maud Pierson, died here in the infirmary of peritinitus (or however you spell it). Her mother and father have been here for about a week. Her mother is an invalid and her father is blind. She was ill two weeks. Her body was taken away yesterday. Wasn't it sad?

Au revoir, Mammy. Are you coming up Thursday? Why don't you bring the kid? (Was taken sick yesterday).

Lovingly,<br>Fan

---

November 11

Dear Daddy,

Hurrah! Prexy has announced that we are to have a holiday the Friday after Thanksgiving, so I can come home on the

29th and stay until the 4th. Isn't that great? And I want the McCurdys to come stay with me.

On Tuesday night I am going to sit on the roof of the observatory to take observations of the meteoric showers, from midnight until two. Won't that be fun? If there is time, forward this letter to Mother.

Lovingly,<br>Fan

---

November 13

My dearest Mother,

This Friday is the first Hall Play, so I can't leave, but I am very anxious to come down from Nov. 24-26, and again from Nov. 29-Dec. 4. I don't see how I am going to manage Mrs. K., but I guess I can jolly her up into giving me permission. The first time I come down, I am going to bring Maude, and I think I would like to bring Mabel Day and Nina Blackmer (they are room-mates). Of course we would have room enough in the house for them all, but I don't see how we could entertain them. I would like to bring them as Mabel and Nina don't have very much pleasure outside of college. Do you believe it might be feasible to have a theatre party either Friday or Saturday night, and take six in the bus and four in the brougham? Please write me what you think.

Sterling Beardsley was up here calling on Eleanor Samson Saturday afternoon.

Au revoir,<br>Fanny

---

November 18

My dearest Mother,

Isabel and Florence McCurdy accept with pleasure our invitation for Nov. 29-Dec. 4. She says, "Nothing could prevent our accepting. Florence says we would both joyfully have whooping cough over again, to be that long with you!" They say *over again,* so that must mean that they have had it. In another part of the letter, Isa says "Whooping cough is no drawback".

So you see, Mother, the girls don't mind the whooping cough at all, and I guess if they don't kiss Helen, it will be all right.

Poor kid! Give her my love.

Must stop now. Head feels better.

Lovingly,<br>Fan

P.S. My dear, *imagine* anybody *marrying* Will Covell. Just think of having to sit down to meals with him and talk to him forever. Oh! law!

Tell Dad that it is certainly time we moved. Harlem is detestable, so many flats! There is an exhibition of Gibson's original drawings at Keppels in 16th street, which it would be nice to go to with the McCurdys.

---

November 23

My dearest Mother,

I went to Mrs. K. this noon. She was right frigid, but when I said that, "Mother and I would both be more satisfied if I could see the doctor again", she gave me my permission. Maude and I will get to the Grand Central at 1.30, have you meet us there, get lunch downtown, go see about my new suit, go to Madame Reilly's and then back to the house in time for dinner.

Then you could have Sterling and Fred to dinner, (if either of them refused, Arthur), and we could go see Julia Arthur in the evening. If Sterling hesitates at first about coming, tell him I'll never forgive him if he doesn't come.

Lovingly,<br>Fan

P.S. Or maybe we should get tickets for Julia Marlowe in *Barbara Fritchie,* or Annie Russell in *Miss Hobbs.*

My dear Mother,

Got a letter from Ethel Boies asking me to go to Scranton after Christmas and stay for a week or ten days. Isn't Ethel a love? What shall I write her? That I shall be charmed to come?

How is the kid? I hope better. Poor 'ittle lambkin!

Evelyn Peverley and Arthur Hyde are engaged to be married. It was announced on Thanksgiving day. Did you ever hear of anything quite like that? And she knows what an ass he is, too.

Lovingly,
Fan

---

December 8

My dearest Mother,

Maude and I went to dinner at the Nelson House with Cousin Robert last night. We had the grandest time. Cousin Robert is a jewel. And then this morning he sent *five* boxes of flowers. One for Maude, one for Mabel Day, one for Marjorie Weills, one for Nina and one for me. Isn't that too nice for anything.

Edward Everett Hale preaches here this morning. Isn't that fine? He was to have preached one Sunday last year, but he forgot to come. I hope he won't forget this year.

I want the new Gibson book, containing the *Pipp* series. Also the Gibson calendar for 1900, so if my aunts want to know what to give me for Christmas, tell them.

I think you might have yielded to the temptation of buying that hat in Helene and Tabors. Which reminds me, don't you think it might be a good plan to take my pink velvet hat and some mink (boa) and have them make it into a larger hat and trim it with the fur?

Yesterday Maude, Grace Bruce and I started out to walk

right after lunch, about 1.45, and walked steadily until 4.15. I think we must have walked 7 miles. It was grand.

Lovingly,
Fan

---

December 18

My dear little bit of a tiny little slip of a kid sister, how is your cough? I hope that by the time I get home, you will be your lovely self once more! Ha! Ha! Next Friday!

What do you want old Santa Claus to bring you. A baby rattle? Or a little nigger doll?

Why don't you write to your big sister, you little bit of a slob! I wish I had you right here on my couch. Wouldn't I maul you. But alas! I must away and don my clothes before the supper bell. "Je vous aime, Je vous adore, que voulez-vous encore?"

Au revoir,
Titter

---

Scranton, Pa.
December 29

My dearest Mother,

Am having *the* time of my life. Can't write you about it. Will have to wait until I see you. The Boieses are *grand*. So is the house and everything. There were shields in my white waist. The woman was talking like a rabbit. Please send the white silk waist too.

The Bachelors is tonight and I am excited to death. I love it here. There are five men staying here and one other girl besides myself. Am awfully busy, so excuse my short note.

Your Fan

64

My dear Mother,

On Wednesday I arrived here and telegraphed you. On Thursday I wrote you. On Friday I wrote you, and Dave forgot to mail the letter until Saturday. On Saturday I wrote you and put a special delivery stamp on it so you would get it Sunday.

Talk about you being uncomfortable, what do you think it makes me, to get letters and telegrams from you all the time, jumping all over me.

I am having the time of my young life, and of course have not had much time to write.

As there is a dance tonight, I cannot take a very early train in the morning. Will probably take the 12 something.

Love to Dad and the kid.

Lovingly,
Fan

---

January 11

Mammy dearest,

For the love of the long lost Charlie Ross, send me some camphor ice. And please don't get it in a card-board box. There's a love.

Have to hand in my elections next week and I don't know what to elect. I am in perfect despair. I feel that whatever I elect, I shall be sorry afterwards. I must choose two subjects from: Greek, Latin, Astronomy, Paleontology. It will probably end up in my taking Greek and Astro.

This is certainly the hardest time of the year at college. The girls are blue and the mornings are dark and exams are coming. But I am cheering up on the thought of February.

Wasn't that awful about the Pulitzer house? What time did you see it burning?

Well, my dear, I must quit. My cold is better but I will not take that horrid medicine of Dr. Burris'. It almost made me actively sick. It seems as if I had been here 2 months instead of 2 days.

Lovingly,<br>
Fan

---

My dearest Mother,

The ice-carnival was beautiful last night. After it was over we had a feast in our room. Will you please have Henry find my skates, clean them, get new straps, and send them to me. I am *all for skating*.

Got a letter from Ethel Boies this morning. She does not know that I am going to the Princeton prom. I am going to surprise her. She said she was going to spend the night of the 8th at Anne Katzenbach's. I do not think that I quite like your note to Mrs. Katzenbach. It sounds terribly stiff. If you really think that you ought to meet her, I think it would be much better for you to call there without writing to her.

Thank you for the black hair-ribbon. I would certainly *not* like to go to the breakfast of the Wadleigh Association.

Nasty night, so did not go to Chapel.

Lovingly,<br>
Fan

---

My dear Mother,

Thank you for the skates. Of course I'll be careful. They never allow the girls to skate on the lake unless it is perfectly safe. Time is going much more rapidly. Exams are approaching almost too quickly, except that it will be nice to get them over with.

By the way, Mabel Day may not be able to come with me on the 2nd. She is trying to sell a little bit of a shanty she owns in Albany. If she does not sell this, she will have to leave college after the exams, and teach for a living, as she has no

66

money. She has to get a position next June anyway, teacher, governess, tutor or something. She asked me if I knew of any such position.

The exams are posted. I have:

Monday — Argumentation
Tuesday — History
Wednesday — Chemistry
Thursday — Greek
Friday — Astronomy

Lovingly,
Your daughter, Fan

---

January 22

My dearest Mother,

Yesterday was the most awful day you ever hope to see. Then last night Maude washed my hair, and when I was drying it, some of the girls came down and read out loud and sewed.

Has Dad gotten tickets for *Sherlock Holmes* for Friday night? What about Saturday afternoon? I think *The Little Minister* would be good, as none of the girls have seen it, *Brother Officers* would also be good, and *Ben Hur*.

Lovingly,
Fan

---

January 23

My dearest Mother,

I got the enclosed letter from Alice Mould today. I don't know what party cape I could send her, but whatever I send, I've got to do it as quickly as possible. I could send her my blue cape lined with fur (and wear my heavy black jacket for a few days), or you could send her one of my capes from home. *If* I am to send her my blue cape which I have here, *please telegraph* me at once. If not, please tend to it yourself. This morning I went to "Cornwallis", and she (after a lot of talking and jollying on my part) gave me leave of absence from Feb. 2 to 4 and Feb. 8 to 12. Also got permission for girls from Feb. 2 to 4.

Have to do Greek. Please decide about Alice and let me know.

Lovingly,
Fan

---

73 Newberry Street
Boston, Mass
January 21, 1900

My dearest Fanny,

Doubtless you will be very much surprised to hear from me at this stage of the game, and from Boston — Nelle and I are both here visiting and will probably stay until Easter.

I have a *great* favor to ask you, but as we are cousins I feel almost certain you won't think I am nervy.

We are both invited to a dance Friday Eve., it is to be very swell, quite the event of the season amongst the crowd of young people we know. We are both all right as to gowns, but we neglected to bring any capes, feeling almost certain that we would not attend any dances.

We are to go on a private car and I wanted to know if I could borrow a party cape — if you have one up at college with you, if you could express it I would willingly pay express charges and would be so grateful to you dear — if you haven't any do you think you could send home for it and then send it to me.

Please try to help me out of my difficulty and answer my letter as soon as you can — some day I will do something to repay you, and now as I have to go downtown will close. Nelle sends love and as for myself I am,

Your loving cousin,
Alice.

68

PERSONAL! IMPORTANT!

My dearest Daddy,

I want to write to you about Mabel Day. She is a grand girl and I was never so sorry for anybody in my life. About a year before she came to college she had mother, father and plenty of money. Then her mother died. So she kept house for her father. Last summer her father died and it was found that it would take all his money and Mabel's too to pay his creditors. She has an older brother, but he has no money and is not much good anyhow. Mabel is an awfully bright girl. She has not money enough to stay at college next semester, but must try to get a position and teach somewhere. She is just about sick, poor girl, and worries all the time. She owns a little bit of a house in some poor part, I believe, of Albany, and if she can sell this, it will bring her in enough money to stay at college until June. She has a customer, who may buy it, and she expects to hear whether he will or not by tomorrow or next day. I believe that Mabel's mother had a mortgage on the house before she owned it and it was never removed, and that is why the customer is not sure about taking it.

Mabel's lawyer is named Rudd of the firm Harrison, Rudd, of Albany.

Now Daddy dearest, Mabel *has got* to come to college next semester. It will break her all up if she does not. And she is *proud*, prouder than anybody I ever saw. That house of hers *must be sold*, and it must be sold by *February 1st*, as that is the end of the semester. If the customer, who has the house in view, takes it, why it is all right. But if he does not, somebody else must.

Now Dad dear, what can be done? If that customer does not buy it, can't you think of somebody who will? If I had enough money, I would. But Mabel must not think I told anybody about this. And I don't dare question her to find out anything more about the house.

Don't breathe a word of this to anybody and if you should do anything about it, keep your *name* out of it.

Forgive me for writing you such a long letter as I know you hate them and believe me

Your loving daughter,<br>Fan

*This letter was sent to Mr. Simpson's office at 97 Fifth Avenue.*

---

My dearest Mother,

Had class meeting yesterday and elected Frances Fenton president for next semester. Most exciting meeting I ever attended. Lots of opposition, etc. Then in the dining room last night we put our table against the one next to ours making a long table, and had a grand dinner party for the old and new officers of the class.

I bought a little ice cream freezer downtown and after chapel last night we made the best lemon water ice you ever tasted.

Mammy dear, will you persuade Dad to buy me a 50 trip ticket (in my name) and send it to me before next Thursday. All the tickets the girls have here have been already engaged for next week. It would really save money in the end because it makes a difference of 90¢ every time I come to New York, and when I do not want to use it, I can rent it to other girls. And they hold good for a year. So please ask Daddy to send me one right away, there's a love.

Must go to Astro. Mabel has not yet heard about her house, tell Dad.

Lovingly,<br>Fan

---

My dearest Dad,

You are a love and a dandy. There is no doubt about it. But the trouble is that Mabel is so *very* proud, that she will not ever let anybody treat her to a dinner at Smith's. So I would not ever *dare suggest* the grand scheme which you planned. So, my dear, the only way out of it that I see is to buy the house. I believe it is not worth much anyway. It is not the one in which they used to live, but one which her mother used to own. So I think Mabel would rather get rid of it than not. Only, if you do buy it, Mabel must never know *who* bought it. Isn't it possible for a lawyer to buy it for you, without your name becoming known to Mabel? And another thing, Dad dear, Mabel is having awfully hard work putting her mind on exams, with this hanging over her. So if she could only get a *telegram* from her lawyer, Rudd, saying that the house was sold the *very early* part of the week, I *know* it would help her to pass her exams.

So you and Cousin Robert are the owners of the Estey Piano Co. Well, I hope you make a success of it.

And we are really going to move to 988 Fifth. I don't quite know what to think. I like the locality but don't like the house. Am pleased to death about the tickets for the theatre and opera.

But, Dad, I am very busy studying for exams, so must say good-bye.

Lovingly your daughter,<br>Fan

---

January 29

My dearest Mother,

You must have had a fine time with your five men last night. Does Mr. Parce still look like Mephistopheles?

I think I would like new revers put on my black coat before I go to Princeton. If Altman's promised it, they would keep their promise. Am going to study hard for exams but may not pass them all. Please don't mind if I don't.

But lovey, I must stop and go to chapel.

Lovingly,<br>Fan

February 4

Dearest Mother,

Arrived safely and no flunk notes yet. They will probably be out tomorrow.

Found a black note from Mary Marshall. *She is back.* I am that crazy to see her, but of course cannot go over to Main tonight.

It makes me homesick, too, to think of moving into that gloomy house. I guess 11 Mt. Morris is not so bad after all. Let's not move! However, I suppose we'll get used to it.

Lovingly,
Fan

---

Cap and Gown Club
Princeton, N. J.
February 9

Dearest Mother,

Here I am, as you see, at the Cap and Gown Club. I was so busy trying to get lunch, when we got here, I did not have time to write. Am getting along beautifully.

Lovingly,
Fan

---

February 15

My dearest Mother,

Isabel McCurdy is coming here to spend a few days with me. Can't you scrape a few things together (such as marsh-mallow cakes, angel cake, a caramel cake, some oranges and grape-fruit, lemons and anything else you think of.) I think if you send it any time tomorrow (Friday) I will get it on Saturday. You will be an angel-love if you do.

Lovingly,
Fan

My dearest Mother,

Will you please send my cards to Miss Halsted and Mrs. Francis Shay Halsted, as I received an invitation to their receptions.

The rubbers came all right, thank you. It was the funniest thing. Friday night I got notice that there was a registered parcel for me. So the next morning I went to the office, and asked for it. I had to sign two or three books and then the man went to the safe and after working a lot of combination locks, he pulled my rubbers out of the safe!

Got a letter from Emery saying that he expected Ethel and Anne to spend the day at Princeton Washington's Birthday. Lucky dogs! Never mind though, *think* of June. Am all for Princeton.

Now why don't you move before my Easter vacation, because during Lent before Easter, it seems to me would be a better time to move than after Easter. Then, as you would need a rest after moving, let's all of us go away somewhere on the 23rd and stay until about the Wednesday of the following week. I think that I would like to go to Atlantic City. That is such a grand place to rest and get feeling well. (If we did think of going to Atlantic City, Daddy ought to write *at once* and engage rooms on the sea at Haddon Hall). I would like to have some girl with me, maybe Maude. Then I want to go back to New York. On the 30th is the Princeton Glee Club concert. And alas! on the 4th I come back here.

Why is my vacation all in Lent? I *loathe* it. Nothing doing at all. The girls send you their love and courteous regards.

Lovingly,
Fanita

---

February 21

Dearest Mother,

Had a grand party Sunday night. Don't be shocked! That

just means that instead of going to the table for supper, eight girls had supper in our room.

Got a letter from Ethel and also from Ann. They expected to go down to Princeton for the day on W's birthday, but they could not get a chaperone.

My very dear Mother, thank you muchly for thinking of such a nice thing as to send us ice-cream. It is most dear of you and I am truly grateful. I will send back the freezer to Mazzeti tomorrow.

Must say au revoir. Please explain to Dad that it is all right for me to go to the Washington's birthday party as a man. Florence McCurdy sent me her knickerbockers, and I am wearing a white waist with frills.

Please tell Dad that I sent my semester bill to his office. Hope he got it all right. Also that Mabel sold that little house of hers and has paid her tuition for the rest of the year.

How about moving, vacation and Atlantic City?

Hurrah! I shall soon have to be getting summer clothes. I am all for summer-time.

I bid you fare-well. Love to Dad and the kid.

Lovingly,
Fan

---

February 26

My dearest Mother,

The play last night was splendid — "Lord Chumley". Lucia Cole took Sothern's part to perfection.

How are you getting along with the 5th Avenue house? Is my carpet all bought? And is the library finished? I hope that Dad will have book shelves *all* the way around the wall of the library. It would look so well.

Yesterday I bought a new Morris chair for $5, and sent the bill to Dad's office.

About plans: you see I don't want to miss the Pr. Gl. Cl. concert on the 30th in New York, so I would only be able to be away a week. If you think it would be worth while, I should love to go to Old Point. Should I ask Mabel Day, Maude Wright or Mary Marshall (who do not expect to go home for vacation)? If you come up here this week we can talk it over then, but I don't think we ought to leave it any longer than that. Must study Chem.

Lovingly,<br>
Fan

---

March 15

My dearest Dad,

Of course I am disappointed about not being able to take all the girls with me to Atlantic City, but I can see that it would cost too much. I don't think that we would spend as much as $55 (which you figured it) on chairs and shows, but still $145 is a good deal of money. I wish that I could go without my brass beds, book-shelves etc., and have them go, as it would do them *all* so much good, physically and mentally. But I suppose that is out of the question.

I am going to ask the girls if they think that they could afford to spend $30 a piece. If any of them think they can (which I don't believe they will) I will let you know and you can telegraph for rooms. Mary is delighted to accept. You are a love, Dad, to let me take anybody. But I must go to chapel.

Your loving daughter,<br>
Fan

---

March 19

My dear Mother,

I am glad that Mary is going with us to Atlantic City. And I do wish that Maude, Mabel, and Nina were going too. I wish that enough money to pay their hotel bill would drop into

75

my lap (they could pay their own fares). Yesterday was Mabel's birthday. I gave her 6 American Beauties.

Well, Mother, I must go to lunch.

Good-bye,<br>
Fan

P.S. Will Howe is going to the Gym Exhibition at Columbia. Why don't you write and ask him if he wants to come to our house to dinner.

---

April 5

My dear Mother,

Trunk is unpacked, curtains up, etc. Wednesday afternoon played basketball in the gym, and today played out in the circle against the freshmen. Have been very busy making out men's cards for Founders. It really is an awful job. I wish we had a nicer boat than the "Hudson Taylor," the "Fanita" for instance. Our party on the boat will consist of 30; and 2 chaperones.

Poor little Mother, I expect you are awfully busy moving, my love. And so the kid is going to have a long sojourn at Atlantic City. She is a gay bird. *Do not* tire yourself out. It will not pay.

Lovingly,<br>
Fan

---

April 6

My Dearest Mother,

What about my bringing a girl down with me for Easter? Of course the house will be awfully upset, and you will be very busy, but I don't believe it would make matters any worse to have a girl sleeping in the other bed in my room and I want to go to the theatre on Saturday anyway. Will you ask Dad to get tickets for some good play. Of course that is if you and Dad won't be too tired.

If you do want me to bring somebody, I think I'll either bring Maude or Frances, or some other Episcopalian.

Well, my dear, I must stop. Today I start training. That means eating certain things etc. Just wrote to the kid.

Lovingly,
Fan

---

April 9

My dearest Mother,

I am in a great quandary what to do. Mrs. Kendrick said that I could not leave college until Friday. I may take the risk and go home on Thursday. Don't above all things write to Mrs. K.!

Our plans are progressing beautifully for Founders. We want to give the men luncheon in our room on Saturday the 28th. Do you think that you could send me a box of food for that festive occasion?

Au revoir. Love to Dad. Don't let him forget to send me Schwill's History of Modern Europe.

Lovingly,
Fan

---

April 11

My dearest Mother,

Please send to me *immediately* the pencils I sorted out and left on the sitting room table (ask the kid about them). Also my Greek translation. It is written on thin sheets of block paper with my name in upper right hand corner. It begins somewhat like this: "Listen to me, as I tell you the argument over again from the beginning." There are probably 7 or 8 sheets. It is very important. I hope it has not been thrown away.

Thank you muchly for the fluffy thing. It was just what I wanted. I have one pair of long gloves here, which are not very decent, but it would seem a shame to wear a new pair that night.

Must stop now. Don't be lonesome.

Lovingly,
Fan

*This was the first letter addressed to 988 Fifth Avenue.*

---

April 23

My dearest Mother,

Here is what we need for the feast:
2 dozen small cakes, marshmallow etc.
bread and lettuce for sandwiches
butter and mayonnaise
pickles, olives, dates etc.
small pies
coffee, loaf sugar
boned chicken
new potatoes (which we are going to cut in thin slices and cook in melted butter, thus making potatoes sauté. Do these have to be boiled or anything like that before we use them? If so will you have them boiled?)
what do you think about sending us up strawberries? I think they would keep, if we got Mother Flett to put them in the icebox in the infirmary. We would probably need 5 boxes.

Love to Dad and kid. Don't forget white shirt waist, dark gray suit and white feather thing.

Lovingly,
Fan

---

April 30

My dearest Mother,

Thank you *very very* much for the grand box. It was the best one I ever saw. All the things you thought of were splendid and the luncheon was a *grand success!* So was the whole thing. The men had the time of their lives and so did we.

And now, alas, it is all over and I begin work tomorrow and my law! How I will have to work.

Am too sleepy to write more tonight.

Devotedly,<br>Fan

---

May 1

Love

Hurrah! I drew a good enough choice to get a double in either Strong or Raymond next year. It was 7th choice in doubles of the girls, who had been in halls this year. Must go to bed.

Devotedly,<br>Fan

---

May 3

My dearest Mother,

We are all just as pleased as we can be. Maude and I chose our room yesterday. It is 209 Raymond, a dandy double. It is on the second floor, facing the west (we could not get an eastern room). And the best of the whole thing is that our crowd is all over in Raymond. We were so afraid that we would be scattered. On our floor are Grace Bruce, Gertrude Barnard, Helen Crum, Frances Fenton and Lou Ramsay. On first are Mabel, Nina, Helen Crosby and Florence Dunning. We have a dandy table made up for next year: Maude, Mabel, Nina, Helen Crum, Gertrude Barnard, Grace B., Clara Holt, Frances Fenton, Lou Ramsay and I.

Isn't it almost too good to be true?

Have a Lit. exam to cram for, so will bid you adieu.

Lovingly,<br>Fan

P.S. Mrs. K. has not called us up about staying out late on Saturday night so I guess that she has not discovered it. Anne

K. wants me to go to Princeton with her on the 12th. Perhaps I can get permission from Mrs. K. What shall I write to Anne? Of course I am wild to go!

---

My dearest Mother,

Please tell Daddy that I am *much in need* of money, as I have just $1.04 left and I have not yet paid for the boat ride on Founders, and I owe dues to several societies here.

I like Daddy's nerve, exchanging our pool table, when I wanted it up at the Lake.

Hurrah! we won! Beat the Freshmen 2-0. Isn't that glorious! I played in the second half, as Theo Hadley got tired.

Just got your letter and I don't understand you at all. If I go to Princeton, and Lake George or Scranton on the 14th, it seems to me I ought to be home once before college closes. Now about the summer. A lot of college girls could come to the Lake in September before college opens. But the trouble is that the Lake is not so gay then, and I probably could not give them as good a time. Then of course I want Mary Banks sometime and the McCurdys. Then I'd like to have a house-party with Ethel Boies, Anne K. and some Princeton men.

So you see, I don't want anything. Now how am I to arrange dates with them? And of course I must visit in Scranton, and Youngstown to see the dear McCurdys. And they won't be happy 'till they get me there either.

Love to all,

Devotedly,
Fan

---

May 12

My dearest Mother,

I forgot to tell you one plan we had, for about four of us (probably Maude, Gertrude and Grace) to go to the dandiest old farm-house we know of near here from June 13th to 16th or 18th. It is the grandest house, 150 years old, right near a big brook and in every way desirable. Of course we girls would have a grand time there. But I must confess that I don't quite see how I am going to work *all* my schemes.

Am very busy this afternoon writing a special topic in Latin, so will say fare-well. Love to *all*.

Devotedly,
Fan

---

May 20

My dearest Mother,

Of course we don't want an evening theatre party so soon after Edma's death. I guess you had better get tickets for a matinee. I have seen *Pride of Jennico* and *Sherlock Holmes*. Is *Lord and Lady Algy* playing?

Saturday morning I suppose there would be some shopping and jumping around down town to do. Then Saturday night I might ask some men in to call. If you see any men I know, ask them. Fred, Frank, Emery, Charley, Joe. Oh! dear, I can't think of any nice men. I guess I don't know any.

Frankly and without hesitation, by all means, come to Princeton with us. I only hesitated the other day, because I thought you would not enjoy yourself very much, but I guess you and Mrs. Katzenbach can get some fun out of it.

Yes indeed the maple sugar came and we have been enjoying it ever since. I clean forgot to thank you for it. I have to go to History now.

Lovingly,
Fan

---

May 27

My dearest Mother,

Just finished basketball. You know we play two 7-minute halfs. In the first half nobody scored, in the second half nobody scored. Lo and behold! it was a tie. The Juniors were

81

very much astonished, as their team had beaten the Freshmen and Seniors. So we had to play a third half. Nobody scored! I played abominably, by the way. So we have to play off the tie on Monday afternoon. But even if the Juniors do beat us now, we have given them a pretty hard tussle.

Last night we had our first Qui Vive meeting and elected the Speaker, Clerk, and Sergeant-at-arms.

The purpose of Qui Vive is: "To promote the art of debate and to gain information on current topics of interest". The members are drawn from every alternate class beginning with 1884. Sometimes we debate against T and M (nobody knows what that stands for!). In March the question was: Resolved, "That England's policy in the Transvaal is justifiable". Qui Vive had the negative and we *won!*

I don't think it will be nearly as soft, pretty and fluffy to finish off the bottom of my lace overskirt with navy lace as it would be to finish it off with a soft ruche of chiffon, mousseline de soie or something of that sort. I wish Madame Reilly could have seen the bottoms of those lace dresses we saw at Altman's. I am all for having the bottom very fluffy.

Will you ask Dad what he would think about my having ten girls at Lake George for the last few days before college opened in September. Even if some of the summer crowd has gone, we could go out on the Fanita, etc. Then we could all come back to college together. Of course if you and Dad *frankly* approved I would have to say something to them about it this Spring.

Lovingly,<br>Fan

---

May 29

Dearest Little Mother,

Am too sleepy to write anything except that I love you a whole heart full and hope that you are quite well again by now.

The game was postponed, but will probably come off soon.

Lovingly,<br>Your Fan.

---

May 31

My dearest Mother,

We played three more halfs, and neither side scored, so now I don't know what will happen.

The girls are delighted with the invitation to Lake George. Maude is waiting to mail this. Will write more later.

Lovingly,<br>Fan

---

June 2nd

Dearest Mother,

We beat the Juniors, 2-1. Isn't that simply great! Your daughter played as a sub for Helen Crosby. I've played in all the match games except the first one against the Seniors. Then I had tonsilitis.

How is the kid, Mother mine? I do hope that she has not got the measles. Oh! I don't believe she has.

Lovingly,<br>Fan

---

June 3

My dearest Mother,

Yesterday was the Senior auction. In the afternoon they had a circus out in the circle, and in the evening a comic opera in the gym. Tonight we had supper club in our room and the box was very useful. It arrived in fine condition and was enjoyed, I can tell you.

Will you ask Dad to get the list of music for the Angelus for April, May and June. I believe they come out monthly.

By the way did I tell you what I have elected for next

83

year? German, Economics, Greek (Thucydides), Theme Course in English, and a course in Nineteenth Century Poetry. Rather hard work!

Well, good-night, Mammy love.

Devotedly,
Fan

Think of next Friday!

---

June 7

My dearest Mother,

Four of my exams are over. That leaves Chemistry Friday morning. Will send my trunk tomorrow. Enclosed here you will find the trunk check.

I take the 11.25 train Friday morning and wish to stay down town and shop all the afternoon. Haven't a whole piece of underwear to my name.

Lovingly,
Fan

## JUNIOR YEAR

Estey Piano Co.
New York City
J. J. Estey — President
John Boulton Simpson — Vice President
Robert Proddow — Treasurer
Stephen Brambach — Secretary
September 24, 1900

Miss Fanny Proddow Simpson
Manager "The Vassar Kids"
My dear Fanny,

I understand the above title is the one you used last week while "starring" Lake George regions. It looks and sounds well.

I must go to Poughkeepsie either this week or next, and would like to know which is your "easy" day, as I can go any day but Thursday.

85

I will be at leisure from 1 P.M. until 6 P.M. so you can arrange for your own pleasure accordingly. I will object to nothing, but upsetting your Dad and a ride to the Lunatic Asylum.

Sincerely yours,<br>Cousin Robert

---

September 25*

My dearest Mother,

Today has been another busy one. In town I got the cutest little tabouret, also curtain rods and other necessary articles.

Mother it is simply *great* over here in Raymond this year, all the girls I like best. We are going to have a great old time. I suppose you are beginning to get busy packing up.

Mabel is in colors again. She is so much brighter and happier than she was last year.

Lovingly,<br>Fan

* *Addressed to*: *Sagamore, Lake George, N. Y.*

---

September 27

My dearest Mother,

It is now 8 A.M. and I have finished breakfast, made my bed, and straightened up the room.

What time do you expect to come through Poughkeepsie on Monday? If I don't have a recitation, I might go down to the station and see you.

The new infirmary is awfully pretty. One of the doctors (Dr. Kimball) is not here this year, and there is the sweetest new doctor, (Dr. Hawley) in her place. I am on the committee for the First Hall Play, [*The Intruder* by Maurice Maeterlinck] which is the most important Hall play of the year. By being on the committee I get a guest seat (the guest seats are all good seats right up in front). So, Mother mine, you must come up for it. I think it is about Thanksgiving time. Au revoir.

Devotedly,<br>Fan

---

September 29*

My dearest Mother,

The flowers from Saratoga were from all the girls who visited us at the Lake. They forgot to put a card in, so I suppose the man thought they were from Grace Bruce, who ordered them.

Cousin Robert is coming up on Monday. Won't that be fun?

I was surprised to hear of your change of plans, especially in regard to your going down on the night boat instead of the train.

As I have two themes to write, must bid you adieu.

Devotedly,<br>Fan

* *Sent to Plaza Hotel, New York, N. Y.*

---

October 2

My dearest Mother,

I have decided to ask Miss Cornwall for permission to go home this Friday. My work on the factory is due on October 12th, so I had better go home this Friday and go to the factory Saturday morning. I would like to bring Maude home if it would not inconvenience you.

I just got your last night's letter. I suppose if you do stay at the Plaza over this Sunday, I can't bring Maude down with me, though it would be lots of fun to have her. Let me know, Mammy dear, whether I'm to go to the hotel or the house, I don't much care which. Also about Maude, whom I think it would do good to get away.

Give lots of love to Dad and ask him why he does not

87

honor his daughter with a letter now and then. He has not
written to me since I have been away.

Most Lovingly yours,
Fan

P.S. You ought to hear me spout German!

---

October 4

My dearest Mother,

Maude and I will be with you at the hotel Friday P.M. It
does not make any difference to us when we start from here,
but time in New York is of the utmost consequence. So unless
you hear to the contrary, expect us at 6.25 at the Grand Central. (It certainly is unfortunate that I have an afternoon
recitation). You did not mention getting tickets for the theatre
on Saturday night. Am crazy to see Freddie Reynolds again, so
you might let him know that we were coming down. In fact
you might ask him to the theatre Saturday night. The trouble
is I don't know what other man would make it pleasant (unless
Will Howe happened to be home).

By the way, my head-light hat is the only one I have here
to wear. Can't you capture me one from the house, my sweetheart?

Love to Dad and the kid.

Devotedly,
Fan

---

October 8*

My dearest Mother,

We arrived safely, feeling very well.

Lovingly,
Fan

* *From now on, addressed to 988 Fifth Ave.*

---

October 8 — later

My dearest Mother,

Will you please send me something to take to make me

sleep at night. Last night I went to bed at ten o'clock dead tired, but the only sleep I had to amount to anything was between three and six this morning. I hate to trouble you, Mother, because I know it will worry you, but I didn't want to go over to Dr. Thelberg and — well I'm not used to being awake at night, and I guess I don't know how to act. Don't worry now, Mother mine, I guess I'll either get over it or get used to it. The two nights I was in New York I slept all right and perhaps I will again tonight, but I just dread bed-time. It was not any kind of pain that kept me awake. I guess I'm used to the high life table at the Plaza.

Au revoir, my love. We found no message to see Miss Cornwall about driving on Thursday.

Lovingly,<br>Fan

---

October 15

My dearest Mother,

My trip this morning wasn't bad at all. I read Economics and German part way up and looked out at the river the rest of the way. The train was exactly on time and I got up here in time for lunch. They had milk toast for lunch which made it very pleasant. Right after lunch I went over to Miss Cornwall. She was awfully nice. Just said that next time I felt ill I should send for her and she would come to me immediately. She gave me an excuse from my lessons and said she hoped I would be quite well again soon. She did not seem to mind when I told her that I came back on condition that I was to go home again if I did not get better.

Don't worry about me, Mother mine. It is quite warm here, but a beautiful day. Love to Dad and the kid,

Devotedly,<br>Fan

89

Mother Mine,

I felt very well all day yesterday. Went to bed at 9.30. Slept from 10 to 12. Then I stayed awake for over an hour, but I was bound I would not take a powder. Went to sleep after 1, and slept till morning. I think I did very well for the first night in a different bed. The girls have been simply grand to me. They have insisted upon my sharing their diet orders until I get one (Maude, Clara and Gertrude have diet orders). They do everything they can for me, and treat me like a queen.

Lovingly,

Fan

---

October 18

Mother Mine,

Last night I slept better than I have yet. It grew much colder here and I am finding comfort in my flannel waist. Hope you'll send my new one soon.

Yesterday noon Miss Cornwall called me up. I could not imagine what I had done wrong, and went to her wondering what she had to say. I went in and said, "Miss Cornwall, I think you wanted to see me". She said, "Yes, Miss Simpson, I want to know how you feel". You could have knocked me over with surprise! She then talked quite a while about my taking things easily and not trying to make up my work yet. She said she had spoken to Dr. Thelberg about me, and wanted me to go speak to her about myself. Not to have her prescribe for me, but so that I could get a doctor's excuse to go home if I did not feel all right. She (Miss Cornwall) was perfectly grand.

Then I went down to Dr. Thelberg and talked to her for a while. She suggested giving me a diet order. So now I order all my meals ahead of time, and can have steak, chops, poached eggs, milk toast, graham and white toast any time I want. Talk about luxury! Mother, Dr. Thelberg also said that if I felt badly any time to come to her, and she would give me an excuse to go home. I could not help thinking of Mrs. K. last year and how disagreeable she was.

Our new green bookshelves and cupboard came home yesterday and I am very disappointed in them. The blooming man painted them a regular bottle green, which looks *awfully* with the rest of the room. And I don't believe it will pay to have anything done to them. The only thing I can see to do is to get some pretty silk which goes with the room and cover the cupboard. Then sell the bookshelves, and get some oak ones. After I'm through with the shelves, we could use them at the Lake in Dad's office or some such place.

I wish Dad could have the shelves made at the piano factory. I want perfectly straight flat planks nailed together. No fancy edges (like my shelves at home) or anything of that sort. Measurements: from one side to the other 2 ft. 6 in.
from top to bottom — 3 ft. 9 in. (all outside measurements)
They are to have *no back at all.*
Distance from floor to bottom — 3 in.
Distance from shelf 1 to shelf 2 — 10½ in.
Distance from shelf 2 to shelf 3 — 10 in.
Distance from shelf 3 to shelf 4 — 9 in.
Distance from shelf 4 to shelf 5 — 7½ in.
Thickness of shelves a little less than one inch.
Making the total height of whole concern about 3 ft. 9 in. Cut out a little place in back 9 inches high for the moulding, so that it will set back against the wall.

These explanations are very elaborate but very exact and accurate. But I must away.

Lovingly,<br>
Fan

---

October 19

My dearest Mother,

It will be fine for you and the kid to come up this Saturday. There is nothing going on up here that I know of. Gertrude Barnard's Mother is going to be here.

Frank won the cup last Saturday and also won another match, for which he received the prettiest prize. It was a golf bag about 4 inches long, in which there were six little after-dinner coffee spoons, with handles shaped like golf clubs. He sent it to me. Wasn't that nice?

Lovingly,<br>Fan

---

October 27

Gee! Mother, but I'm glad it's Friday. I just couldn't study another bit this week. I never did have so much to do. This afternoon I have to go to Hall Play rehearsal. (I have been every night this week, and will have to go every night for the next three weeks.) Tonight we give the Freshmen a Halloween Party. Everyone has to go in Mother Goose costume. Grace, Gertrude and I are going as the butcher, the baker and the candle stick maker. I'm the candle stick maker.

Tomorrow morning both before and after my written lesson, I go to rehearsals and in the evening there is a Republican Mass Meeting.

Why don't you get tickets for the theatre for us for Saturday night, and I could ask Emery, Frank Linen, Fred or some of those men.

If you think it would be a good plan, why don't you telephone them and ask if they can come. Also ask what plays they have seen. Their phone number is 95 B., Englewood.

Am crazy to see my pictures and curtains. Do you think they will be up by next Friday? Mammy, if you decide to ask the McCurdys, telephone them right away, won't you, Honey? You had better put their number down on the list.

Ever lovingly,<br>Fan

October 28

Many happy returns of the day, my dearest Mammy, and best wishes for your birthday. I wish this note could get to you today, but alas! it can't.

Mammy dearest, doesn't it seem too strange to be true that Frances has a dear little baby of her own. I am so glad that they are both all right. I am perfectly crazy to see "it". Guess I'll go over to Brooklyn next Saturday, while the McCurdys are at their fitting (they probably have one). Mammy, don't you want to ask Dad to have some flowers sent to Frances with my card?

I was surprised to hear that Ethel was in New York. Oh! I do hope that her mother won't be pig-headed. Why don't you get some tickets for *L'Aiglon* for Thanksgiving night? You have to get them so long in advance.

Lovingly,<br>Fan

---

October 29

My dearest Mother,

This morning I got a letter from Mrs. Warren. She said that Frances had a *very* hard time, but was doing nicely when she wrote. She said the baby was the sweetest thing imaginable.

I am so glad that the McCurdys are coming. Now, about plays. I want tickets for Saturday night, you understand. Perhaps *Henry V* would be the best, but I am not much for it. I don't like the play and I am not at all crazy about Mansfield. *San Toy* at Daly's is apt to be amusing, though of course not very deep. *The Greatest Thing in the World* might be good, though I don't know much about it. If the McCurdys have not seen *A Royal Family* I have not the slightest objection and would really like to see it again. What about Crossman in *Mistress Nell?*

If Julia Marlowe or Mary Mannering are in town, by all

means get tickets for one of them. I'll ask the men to dinner at 6.15. Do you think that will be all right?

As for sleepless nights, I did not sleep well last Wednesday night when I had taken a big dose of salts, but since then I have slept very well indeed.

Love to Dad and kid.

Devotedly,

Fan

---

October 30

My dearest Mother,

Yesterday afternoon some book shelves arrived. They are unfinished, having neither paint, varnish nor stain on them. Just plain boards. What does that mean, am I to have them finished here? The size etc. is just what I want.

Lovingly,

Fan

---

October 31

Mother Mine,

Please thank Dad for the tickets for *Mistress Nell.* I am glad you got them for that, if Aunty Mary said it was very good. The reason why I hesitated about it was because it was at the Bijou, and there are not usually good plays there.

Say, I hear there is going to be a parade in New York on Saturday, and all the stores will be closed. Isn't that a shame? I did want to do some shopping.

Poor little Mammy, I'm so sorry you didn't feel well yesterday, but I hope you are better today. The weather has been so horrid lately I just hate it.

Lovingly,

Fan

November 5

My dearest Mother,

When I got back this morning I found that we had had a cut in English, so I did not miss as many recitations as I thought I would. Right after lunch I went over to the Able General's office. She was very pleasant, gave me my excuse I missed for recitations without a murmur. Then I went to the doctor's office, jollied her up and got a diet order for ten days, so I am still living in ease and luxury.

Poor little Mammy, I know what a hard time you must be having with your tooth, and wish I was there to help you, though I don't know what I could do for you. Give Dad my love and don't let him worry too much. (By the way, a trip-ticket would be most acceptable.) Also tell him that I am sending him my paper about his factory that he wanted to see. Please ask him to send it back.

Lovingly,
Fan

---

FACTORY REPORT FOR ECONOMICS A.
by Fanny P. Simpson

Visited factory October 6th, 1900

1.  Factory is located in New York City, corner of Southern Boulevard and Lincoln Avenue. Population of New York is 3,654,000. Could not find out population by nationalities. Transportation facilities, both rail and water. There are all kinds of other industries in the city. Trade unionism, an open question, strong in some trades and not recognized at all in others.

2.  Estey Piano Company. It is a stock company, because that is the most modern way of carrying on business and secures a perpetuity in the continuance of the business in case one of the owners of the business should die and because of the limited liability of investors. The company has three directors, who are

also the president, treasurer and secretary. It was established in 1885. Form of organization has not changed recently.

3. Amount of capital, $200,000. Capital is the amount of money actually used in the transaction of the business (value of factory not included). Value of factory, $235,000. Value of annual product, $215,000. Approximate annual wages bill, $74,000. High grade pianos made. Percentage of cost due to wages, 62%. Amount of annual product, 1000 pianos. Pianos sold for from $200 to $600 (wholesale).

4. There are employed 120 adult men, no women, and 17 boys (from 16 to 21 years old). There are 14 different kinds of employees:

7 varnishers
7 bellymen
3 stringers
9 finishers
13 fly finishers
45 case makers
21 polishers
8 regulators
3 tuners
2 engineers
6 porters
8 mill-men
1 driver
1 watchman

The number employed does not vary much. In depressions the employees have been put on half time. No adult man receives under $5 per week. 2 adult men receive $5-$6. 4 adult men receive $6-$7. 114 adult men receive over $7. 13 boys receive under $5. 4 boys receive $5-$6. Almost all of the employees are paid by piece. Piece work is preferred because results are better. Rates of wages are determined by what other employers are paying, by the market price of the product and in an attempt to fix a fair day's pay. Wages have not changed recently. Don't know about nationalities of employees.

5. Muscular strength required only in rubbing and polishing cases and in putting in wrest plank and iron plate. Not much skill required, but particular attention to details necessary. There is no system of apprenticeship. It takes from three months to four years to learn the work, according to the branch. The workers are a comparatively permanent force, because the amount of production changes very little. The workers remain in about the same grade, as there is but one in each branch of work.

6. The work is divided into a great many different parts, because by subdivision of labor the workers in each branch become more expert. There are 18 distinct processes. Pianos were never (as far as I can make out), made by one workman. Pianos are not now made by any other than the factory method.

7. There is only one kind of machinery (wood-working machinery). No recent improvements in machinery have been made, which would throw people out of employment. There are no women and children employed for machine work. No automatic machinery is used.

8. There are many establishments making pianos in the vicinity, because there is a very good market for them there. There are no connected or subordinate industries. There are no particular disadvantages in being near other piano factories, but it is advantageous in that there is a good market for supplies. The factory was originally located here because the owners were residents in the city. No work is sent out from the factory to be partly finished at home.

9. This establishment is of medium size compared with other factories in the country. This concern is carried on on a conservative basis and aims to meet a safe, legitimate demand and thereby avoid the many disadvantages of over-production.

10. The profits are increasing slightly, because experience is

making management more capable. Profits are labor, materials and all other items under head of expense (as for instance, cost of mending machinery), subtracted from the gross receipts. Interest on capital and salaries of owners are distinguished from profits as a matter of book-keeping. They are fairly satisfactory. This does not lead to an increase in those engaged in the business. It does pay to run when practically no profits are made. The business is very steady. It is subject to sharp competition. It is not affected by trusts. It is not protected by tariff, because foreign pianos will not stand this climate. Its goods are sold to jobbers. Much credit is given, from 30 days to 2 years. Stock is manufactured to meet demands, as they come along. The establishment manufactures for the United States, Germany and Australia.

11. Employees work 58½ hours per week. They worked 52 weeks last year. The factory is very pleasant, well lighted and well ventilated. The machinery is well guarded. The elevators are automatically protected. The occupation is a healthful one. No processes are carried on in damp, dusty, or very hot rooms. No chemicals dangerous to health are used. One minor accident last year. Operatives carry their outer clothing into the work rooms. The wages are paid weekly in cash. There are no fines or expenses connected with the work that are a real deduction from wages.

12. Houses of the employees are not owned by the establishment. The operatives are apparently contented. The last strike took place about eight years ago. The strikers wanted reduction of hours. Result, no change in hours. There are trade unions among employees to a very limited extent, because many of the employees have some money accumulated and refuse to join unions. The proprietors think that labor organizations are all right, if they are carried on in the interest of the men and not of agitators. The factory is subject to factory laws. Such legislation, especially in regard to factory inspection is thought well of by the proprietors. The establishment

had never tried profit-sharing or other peculiar plan. There is no benefit or insurance fund.

There is very little drunkenness among operatives. Don't know about vice or immorality. Very difficult to find out how factory is regarded by operatives and people of the town. I did not talk privately with any operatives.

---

November 6

Mother mine,

McKinley was elected *here* today by an overwhelming majority. 441 votes for McKinley, 61 for Bryan. We think that McKinley has defended himself well against charges of imperialism by the Democrats. I am all for McKinley! I hope that the United States will vote likewise. The returns will be telephoned up here to the college. At 9.30 we have our band (playing on combs etc.) march through all the corridors. And when the returns come in, we are going to parade all over the campus. (that is, if McKinley is elected).

Later. Have one Bismuth capsule left. Am glad Dad's vote helped to carry New York State. Hurrah for Bill McKinley!

Lovingly,
Fan

---

November 7

My dearest Mother,

This morning we all formed lock step and marched into the dining room to breakfast, singing.

"Rah! Rah! Rah! for Bill McKinley
Rah! Rah! Rah! for dear old Bill. etc." It was really very exciting.

Just write to Mrs. Boies as if I had not written to Ethel weeks ago. (Because she might wonder why Ethel had said nothing to her about it). Say the usual thing, and be just as sweet as possible.

Mrs. H.M. Boies, 530 Clay Avenue, Scranton, Penna.

I don't know quite how to decide about what night to go to the theatre. If we go to Anne's on Friday, Thursday and Saturday are the only nights left. Saturday evening is so Jewy.

I suppose Dad is rejoicing because McKinley was elected.

Lovingly,
Fan

---

November 14

My dear Mother,

Wouldn't Mrs. Boies *jar* you? Never did I hear such a snippy little note. Mother, it will be the disappointment of my life, if that woman does not let Ethel come for Thanksgiving. And you know there is really no reason for her refusing, except just a whim. And they say that she never takes back anything that she has once said. She has no interest in Ethel's happiness at all. I am glad that *my* mother is not like that.

Is there anybody you would like to bring up to the play on Saturday. Aunt Mary or Aunt Esther or Mrs. Van de Water might enjoy it. It is one of *the* functions of the years, all the alumnae coming back, and there being general excitement. I have secured two *good* guest seats right up in front. Maude has a seat right next, so she can tell you all about who the girls are. Bring somebody. I don't want to waste the seat. I was going to suggest that you bring Eloise, but she is going to the game at Princeton. That child! It makes me feel about 100 years old.

Lovingly,
Fan

---

November 16

My dearest Mother,

Isn't Mrs. Boies the biggest old pill! Imagine having a mother like that. Poor little Ethel!

Mother, I think I will go over and telephone to Mary Banks in Albany, and explain about how much I want her to

100

come. I find that I can get three guest seats, so if Mrs. Van de Water would like to come, I should love to have her.

I thought it would be nice for you to stay at college, and sleep in my room. If Mary comes she could sleep on the couch, and either Maude or I could sleep on Nina's couch. Then if Mrs. V. comes, Maude could give up her room and sleep on Gertrude's couch. We could have breakfast in the room Sunday morning (as we sometimes do), making coffee, scrambling or poaching eggs, getting toast, taking all the time we want until church. Lou Ramsay kept her mother in her room for two nights, and nothing happened. It would be nicer than going down town at night. However, just as you say.

Lovingly,<br>Fan

---

November 21

My dearest Mother,

Got a letter from Helen Halsey this morning, asking me to spend Friday night the 30th with her. She said, "we are going to have a 'tea' and then there is a dance later at a little hall in East Orange. The tea is properly speaking my coming out, but that word always makes me shiver. So unless you consider it too much of a bore, Fan, dearest, please do come — as early as you can on Friday — and help me make my bow to society. However it's not going to be very formal or stiff."

That is what Helen said, Mother, and whatever Helen says, I guess it's going to be formal enough. Mary says East Orange things always are. A tea and a dance later means a high neck gown for the tea and low for the dance. My white lace dress will be very pleasant for the dance, but I certainly do want a new one for the tea. Mammy, I've got to go to New York next Saturday to see about it. I am *pretty sure* I can work Cornwallis to let me take the 8.14 Saturday morning arriving at Grand Central station at 10. Then I could see about my dress and come back either Sat. night or Sunday afternoon in time for Supper Club. You might write Reilly I'd be there about 10.30 or else we'd go to Altman's.

What do you think about getting tickets for *The Gay Lord Quex* at the Criterion for Thanksgiving afternoon. *Life* says it's very good. Can't you get 10 tickets, and then give some up afterwards if I don't want them all.

Genevieve gives a tea tomorrow for caste and committee, and Thursday night we have a dinner at Smiths.

Good-bye,<br>
With love,<br>
Fan

---

November 22

My dearest Mother,

The Able General was as docile as a lamb. Handed out my excuse for Nov. 24-25 with hardly a murmur.

I think a white broadcloth trimmed with lace would be most effective and stunning. I don't know how Helen would like it, as she will probably wear white; but I guess she won't care, as mine will probably be a creamier white than hers, and most likely a different style dress anyway.

Mammy dear, you give me a fit, always writing to me on 988 Fifth Avenue paper. You must have used up 2 or 3 quires writing to me on it. I wish you'd purchase some plain paper and write to me on that.

Mammy, I have just asked Maude, Helen Crum, Mabel, Dickie, Nina, Maude Cartwright (Nina's friend) and myself. That makes 7 of us. Unless some of these refuse, I guess I won't ask anybody else, because that would make too many. Oh! law, that leaves out Clara Holt, Florence Dunning, Helen Crosby and Frances Fenton.

Forever yours,<br>
**Fan**

November 25

My dearest Mother,

Got here at college just in time for Supper Club. I hope Dad's Traders business turns out all right. Don't let him worry about it*.

The tables were a great success! Maude has just come back from Chapel and we now have to wash up. That is not the nicest part of it.

By the way, Mother, don't you think it might give me a better figure, if my new white dress were made larger across the bust. You see my corsets are so low they do not fill it out very much, and perhaps if I had the bust made larger, and then wore either my high corsets or a ruffled chemise, it would look better. However, just as you think.

Yours,

Fan

*Mr. Simpson was one of the directors of the Trader's Fire Insurance Company. The Board included John Jacob Astor, Chauncey Depew, Edwin Gould, and others. Unknown to most of these directors the annual statements falsified the amount of cash in the bank, overstated by 50 percent the premiums collected, and understated the losses in the same proportion. Mr. Simpson feared he might have a large fine and/or be imprisoned. The newspapers gave the fraud much publicity but as was generally the case in such matters, the directors were not implicated.*

---

December 6

My dearest Mother,

Enclosed you will find one of my cards. Will you please ask Dad to wrap up the tobacco pouch he will find in my desk, put the enclosed card with it, and mail it to Mr. Emery Katzenbach.

3 South West Brown
Princeton, N.J.

Thanks very much.

I am not too busy to tend to my hair!

Goodbye for present,

Fan

---

December 7

My dearest Mother,

Mabel is back in the infirmary again with more cold. I don't believe it is just cold, or she would get better. I think she ought to have either a doctor from town or an Albany doctor.

Clara is also in the infirmary with a high fever, bad headache etc. I rather think they fear typhoid. Isn't that just too bad! I just hate to have the girls ill.

Love to Dad and the kid,

Lovingly,

Fan

---

December 8

My dearest Mother,

Dr. Thelberg has requested the girls not to go to New York this week, as there is smallpox there. Is that so? Guess you'd better have the family vaccinated. Mabel is out of the infirmary. Have not heard how Clara is today. Have to go over to Phil. Hall now, and decorate for the German. We are having a Japanese German with lanterns, umbrellas etc. Grace Hecker went to New York to get the favors.

Love to Dad and the kid.

Lovingly,

Fan

---

December 9

My dear Mother,

The German last night was lots of fun. Genevieve led, dancing with Grace Hecker.

Clara has a trained nurse. They telegraphed for her father. The doctors won't say what's the matter with her, but we all rather think it's typhoid. Her poor sister who is a freshman, is awfully cut up. I am so sorry for her.

I got a note from Helen Halsey asking me to spend the night of the 27th with her in East Orange, and the 28th also if I could. She is going to give a dance at the Essex County Country Club (the engraved invitation came this morning). I am just crazy about it. She is going to have Stella and H. Warren (the latter more to pay back what she owes than because she wants her, I imagine). On the 28th is another dance of the series, to which I went the last time I was in Orange.

Mammy guess I'd like a new dress for Helen's ball. It will probably be a *very swell* affair. Engraved invitations! I suppose I'll have to write an acceptance, as it says R.S.V.P. It is worded "Mr. and Mrs. G. E. H., Miss H. request the pleasure of Miss S's company on Thurs. Eve." etc. Shall I write: Miss S. accepts with pleas. Mr. and Mrs. G. E. H. and Miss H.'s invitation. That sounds so funny with all those names.

I am engaged in making a corset cover for Mary Banks for Christmas. Won't that be pleasant?

As ever yours,
Fan

---

December 11

My dear Mother,

Went to see Miss C. about getting off on the 20th. She said she would have to think it over, and would send me word tomorrow. She has absolutely no mind of her own.

Have not heard how Clara is today, but yesterday the last thing I heard was that her fever had gone down. I *do* hope she'll pull through without a siege of it.

Too bad about my fuzzy cape, but how was I to know that the mice would eat it up, if I put it in the bottom drawer. I am awfully sorry that it was destroyed as I am quite crazy about it.

Lunch bell just rang. Goodbye. Just heard that Clara had a pretty good night last night. Love to all.

As ever,<br>Fan

---

December 12

My dearest Mother,

Am pleased to death that I can get off Thursday. Cornwall's a pippin!

As I suppose, from all accounts, I shall have to be vaccinated the moment I reach New York, I think it would be a good plan for me to be vaccinated here tomorrow and then I could have a week to get over it before vacation.

This afternoon I am going down town to start on my Christmas shopping. I want to give away some books, but I think it would be much cheaper to get them at Wanamakers (where Dad has a discount), or at Macy's, than in Poughkeepsie.

Yes, indeed, I treat my hair continually. You may expect to see a luxuriant growth, when next you see me. Must stop now.

As ever yours,<br>Fan

---

December 14

My dearest Mother,

Mammy, I'm going to give you something "awful nice" for Christmas, but you don't know what it is. Say, what does the kid want? And that reminds me, I must send you a list of what I want. My wants are not very extensive this year, as I have already gotten so much for my room. I'd like a desk chair and a stool effect for my tea table, but I most think I might like to pick them out myself.

Guess I'm going to be vaccinated tomorrow on my leg. They are vaccinating people right and left here. You never saw anything to beat it. Everybody that is going through New York.

I am now going to read aloud to some girls, who are sewing.

Many happy returns of the day (the 12th) to Daddy. By the way, how about the "Traders?"

Most lovingly,
Fan

---

December 15

My dearest Mother,

The German went off most successfully last night. The girls were crazy about the favors, and I did my best with the figures. I was tired so I stayed in bed this morning and had a meal order, getting up just in time for church. Tonight they had the Christmas music, it was *perfect*. You know the choir dresses in white, and all the lights in the body of the chapel are turned out. It is most effective.

Mammy dear, goodnight. Daddy dear, the same. Also the kid.

Your,
Fan

---

December 16

My dearest Mother,

It was "awful good" to hear your voice on the telephone.

My vac. has not begun to take yet, but I 'spect I'll go limping around the campus pretty soon, and perhaps I'll have to come home on a crutch.

Have you planned about my dress yet? Point d'esprit, I think you said. If my vac. takes so that I can't go to recitations, I'll try to get permission to come home, as there would not be any use in staying. Goodnight, dear.

Lovingly,
Fan

107

December 18

Mother dear, dearest,

Enclosed find my trunk check! Hurrah! Doesn't it make it pleasant? Clara much better today. Am *very busy, busy, busy*.

Yours,

Fan

---

January 9, 1901

Dearest Mother,

Maude and Mabel are not back yet. The schedules for next semester are up, and everything I want comes early Monday morning and late Friday afternoon.

Mammy, I've got a slight cold on my chest. I wouldn't tell you about it, but I don't want to go to Dr. Thelberg. What shall I do for it? Now don't worry and *don't* write to Miss Cornwall or I'll *never* tell you anything again. If it gets worse, I'll get permission to come home.

Hope your Whist Club was fun.

Lovingly,

Fan

---

January 10

My dearest Mother,

This morning my cold is *better,* all except my voice, which is not as beautiful as it used to be. Last night I rubbed my chest with camphorated oil and put flannel over it, and then took lots of whiskey and quinine.

Yours as ever,

Fan

---

January 21

My dearest Mother,

Arrived safely, and am feeling very well thank you. It did my cold great good to go home. Clara Holt goes home tomorrow. Have very little German to make up. Have not found out about the rest of my things yet. Went to the doctor's office and got excused for all the gym and chapel I missed.

Doesn't it seem funny? All my friends are getting married, and some even have babies.

I would very much like Dad to send me a box of oranges.

As ever,
Fan

---

January 26

Dearest Mother,

This morning I got a letter from Marie, saying that she and her mother were going to Washington on February 4th. Mr. Wigmore (the officer who asked *her* down) wrote Marie that there was to be a big hop on the 8th. So she writes me that if I can come down for that hop, she and her mother will meet me at the depot in Washington, and take the very best of care of me. She says nothing about how long she wants me to stay, but I suppose over Sunday.

I would probably have to go down to Washington on Thursday the 7th, and would most likely miss Thursday, Friday and Monday up here. Now it won't matter a bit about my work, as it will be in the next semester, but *what* about Miss Cornwall, our Able General? Of course I ought to write Marie as soon as possible, so I'll have to get up my nerve to go ask Miss C.

Maude was just elected Speaker of Qui Vive for next semester. (That's the same as president you know) In Qui Vive's March debate with T. and M., the question will be: "Resolved, that a defensive alliance between Great Britain and the United States would be for the best interests of the United States." I don't know which side we will have. In December we lost. We had the affirmative, "That a single tax on land values would be better for the U.S. than the present system of taxation."

Arthur's family are just about as stuck on him, as he is on himself. Well, I wish him and his wife joy.

There's going to be an ice carnival tonight and we're going to make coffee and creamed chicken afterward.

As ever yours,
Fan

---

January 30

Dearest Mother,

I have just come from Miss Cornwall and she is a perfect old pill! She hemmed and hawed and said I'd been away a good deal, and all that kind of foolish talk. Finally she told me to come see her tonight after chapel, and she would tell me whether I could or not.

Econ. this morning was awfully hard, but I guess I scraped through somehow. I am now cramming for German and Greek tomorrow morning. I am going to ask Miss Mc-Curdy to let me go into Greek 15 minutes early. If she does I can get out at 12.35. But if she doesn't, I can't get out until 12.50, and then I'm afraid I couldn't make the 1.05 train. So you see I can't let you know for sure when I'll get there.

It is snowing hard. Hope it won't be a blizzard.

Oh! Mammy!, if Cornwall won't let me go, I'll be *furious*. I didn't tell her I was going home tomorrow, and I'm not going to. I'll say I took it for granted you didn't need to get permission as everybody went away and anyway she won't know the difference.

Lovingly,
Fan

---

February 8

Dearest Mother,

Right after lunch went over to the "Able General's". I

went in and said, "Miss Cornwall, I came to tell you that I have to give up my Washington trip after all. I received word yesterday that the regiment there has been ordered to the Philippines, so that there won't be any dance". She said, "I suppose you're heart-broken, but I think it's probably better for you that you couldn't go."

The old pill!

Our table and the table next to us go for a sleigh ride tomorrow night. Shakespeare sleigh ride had been postponed to Wednesday.

Guess I'll get to work on my 5 recitations for Monday.

Lovingly,<br>Fan

---

February 10

Dearest Mother,

We had a great old time on the sleigh ride last night. 16 of us went. Started at 7.30 and ended up at 9 o'clock at Mrs. Cary's where we had waffles, cake and coffee.

The third Hall Play (in French) comes some time before Easter, and the 4th after Easter. I am to be on the committee for the 4th. Ella McClenahan is chairman. I suppose you had a great time at your dinner Friday night. How was your dress? I'm such a fool. I left my shampoo stuff in New York.

Yours lovingly,<br>Fan

---

February 13

Dearest Dad,

Thank you very much for the "Jevons". I guess I won't need any of the other Economics books.

Now about the Greek books, I don't know what to do. As it is I have to study my Greek in the library 3 times a week, often staying over there in the evening. There is always an awful scrap for the books and you sometimes have to wait a

111

long time to get them. If I order them through the office I can probably get them for about $2.80 apiece.

It seems a lot to pay but I guess I'll do it because it means such a great saving of time and trouble to me. I can use my trip-ticket money.

When are you and Cousin Robert coming up? Goodbye, dear Dad. Why don't you ever write to me?

Your loving daughter,
Fan

---

February 15

My dearest Mother,

Do you know, I like my schedule more and more. Of course Monday is an awful day, but then I'm so glad when it's over, and it really means a lot of the work done.

Tell the kid her letter was fine. What made Dad get 5 horses?!

Mammy, I am just discouraged about my hair. I have not put the stuff on for the past week as I *cannot stand* the nastiness of it. My hair is the worst looking stuff you ever saw and still coming out, so I'll have none at all soon.

Helen Crum and her mother are going to Europe in June, sailing on the 15th. I am crazy to go abroad. You ought to hear Helen; she can think of nothing else.

Helen Crosby is on the committee for the 3rd Hall Play, (March 23rd, in French). She told me to write and ask you, if you would come to it and occupy her guest seat.

We are reading aloud *The Woman in White*. It is not very trashy. Have you read it?

Lovingly,
Fan

---

February 20

Dearest Dad,

I would just love to have you come up for Washington's

Birthday with Mother and the kid, and I am very anxious to have you see all the girls, the campus, my room, etc. But really, I think it would be better if you could come some other time, say with Cousin Robert. You see, I intended to take Mother and the kid to dinner with me here in Raymond, and of course I would not be allowed to take you, as some of the girls are dressed as men. There is no chapel. In the evening there is an entertainment in Phil. Hall, to which you would not be allowed to go.

So you see, either you would not see any of us at dinner or during the evening, or else we would all have to give up the entertainment.

Dad, it is unfortunate that you happen to be a man at these times, but I would so much rather have you up here, when I could take you to dinner and spend the evening with you.

Well, dear, I must go to lunch (such as it is).

Many many thanks for the suit, Daddy mine, you are *one love!*

Yours,<br>Fan

---

February 25

Dearest Mother,

After we left you, we walked back to college. It took us about fifty minutes and was simply perfect, the air was so delicious. I studied the rest of the morning. After lunch was a Qui Vive debate. It was a funny one, the subject being — "Resolved — that pigs should have wings".

You don't know how much I enjoyed having you all up here, and only wish you could have stayed over Sunday. The only thing I was sorry about was that Dad had to stay in town Friday night. The kid was so good she'll have to come up again in the Spring and stay 2 or 3 days. I'd give her a good time.

Well, goodbye Dearie,

Yours as ever,
Fan

---

February 26

Dearest Mother,

I have not heard a word about taking Dad up in the room or keeping the kid all night, so you see it was quite safe.

Forgot to tell you that Mabel has sold her house. Couldn't get *nearly* what she thought it was worth, but was forced to sell it, a suit or something I believe. She is in the infirmary now, poor girl. She is a pippin!

Lovingly,
Fan

---

March 1

Dearest Mother,

Have been looking over the theatres and find that *Captain Jenks of the Horse Marines* would probably be good. Then there is *Mrs. Dane's Defense, To Have and to Hold,* and *The Lash of a Whip.* The last is at the Lyceum. We have not seen anything, so I guess tickets for anything will please us.

At last I've got my *Sophocles* that I've been trying for so long. At least it's to come tomorrow (unless it's an idle dream).

Love to all,
Fan

---

March 2

My dearest Mother,

I expect Dr. V. will have the grandest time in Washington. I wish I was going to be there for the inauguration. Some girls from here have gone down for all the festivities, the ball, etc.

It certainly would be nice for the kid to learn to ride. I I am crazy to ride myself, and wish I could do it at the Lake this summer.

Love to all,
Yours Fan

---

March 5

Mother! If I ever ask another man to do anything, my name is mud. Theo wrote an acceptance, but Arthur cannot come. The latter has been away and used up all his cuts, so now he cannot get permission to leave. What on earth shall we do? I can't think who to ask, except Frank Linen or Dickson Torrey, and as Frank has not written me in a long time, I don't want to ask him and Dickson probably could not get off. For the love of the long lost, do get another man, Mammy mine.

Go out in the street and ask anybody!

Yours lovingly,
Fan

---

Estey Piano Co.
Southern Boulevard, near Harlem Bridge
New York City
March 6

My dear Fanny,

Your telegram received, and as women rule the world, I can only bow to the will of the mighty and change the day from Friday to tomorrow, and I will be at the Music Store at 11 o'clock to receive the "Galaxy of Beauty and Brains" when they arrive.

Sincerely your
Robert the Cousin

---

March 6

Dearest Mother,

Hope you telephoned Joe. I don't know why I did not

115

think of him before. And Pierpont is a fine idea, as he's in Mr. Scranton's office, so near at hand.

Mammy, Stella has asked me to be a bridesmaid at her wedding. I am just crazy about it! Must go to Psych.

Yours with love,<br>Fan

---

March 11

Dearest Mother,

Helen, Florence, my new hat and I all arrived at college safely. Mammy dear, I do hope your cold is better. Do take good care of yourself, Mammy, and also of Dad. I am worried about him having so much headache. Why don't you take him away now, and let me join you later. You can insist on the kid dropping school.

Yours devotedly,<br>Fan

---

March 13

Dearest Mother,

Got a letter today from Ethel Boies from Palm Beach. It seems to me that everyone I know is at Palm Beach: Helen Warren, Ethel, Marie Whitmore, Sterling Beardsley, Jim Blair, Mortimer Fuller and many others. Ethel leaves next week for Cuba, Nassau, etc. I wish we could take a trip together during vacation. I don't know where I would like to go, maybe Old Point Comfort. It's too late, and I have not got enough time to go very far south.

Have to go to gym. I'll have to go almost every day for a while to make up my cuts.

Yours most devotedly,<br>Fan

116

Dearest Mother,

My gray coat and skirt arrived yesterday. They had put "Please deliver at once" on the package, so the express office in town telephoned out to me that there were some flowers for me, did I want them sent up by special messenger. So it cost 45c extra to get that suit up yesterday morning.

Am glad the kid is having such a good time over Sunday. That little thing with a dress suitcase is too funny!

The Senior Junior debate came off last night. Grace and Gertrude were simply fine. The Seniors won, but they really did not have nearly as good a debate as we did. One of the judges, Prof. Phelps of Yale, turned out to be an intimate friend of some seniors (which is not allowed). The Seniors' speeches were more flowery but proved nothing. Lots of the instructors here have said that we surely should have won. I felt so sorry for poor little Grace and Gertrude, they worked so hard.

Now about Old Point Comfort, whom shall I take along? I can't help but think it would do Mabel good. Of course she would refuse at first, on account of not having any clothes, but I might be able to persuade her out of that. Do advise me. In one way I want Mary most, but still what shall I do, Mabel's cough still being so bad.

Lovingly,<br>Fan

---

My dearest Mother,

Isabel and Florence McCurdy are coming up on Saturday for the Hall Play. I am going to try to keep them over Monday, for Supper Club Sunday night. You have not forgotten that you are going to send me a box for it, have you? There will be ten of us all told.

Now about Old Point! It won't be nearly as much fun

there Holy Week as Easter Week, but I suppose you would not be away on Easter Sunday for anything. A week seems too short, when you have to take out two days for travel. I could be away all of Easter week, but if we did not leave until Easter Monday, that would give us a shorter time still. I tell you what let's do. Let's leave as soon as college closes and go by boat. I am crazy about it! Then we could see how we would like a sea voyage. Then if we like it, let's stay all Holy Week *and* Easter Week. We could go to church down there, and it would do *Dad lots of good.* He needs it for his health. And it would also invigorate the rest of the family. Do let's!

About Mabel, if we had different beds we could sleep in the same room, and I would just love to see her get better. Still, I think I'll ask Mary. Oh! law, Mammy what shall I do?

Prof. Dwight is the Prof. of Geology. I have him twice a week, and he really knows all about fossils. His wife was very ill last week. She had her leg amputated, but died on Thursday. I feel so sorry for poor old Prof. Dwight.

To think of Marjorie having a daughter. What is everybody coming to?

Well Mammy, I guess I'll have to stop now. Do read this carefully and answer everything, whether it is a question or not.

Don't you *ever* expect to be away from St. Andrews on Easter?!

Love to all.

Yours most devotedly,<br>Fan

---

March 22

Dearest Mother,

Well, of all hopeless families the Simpsons are the most hopeless. They just get in a *rut* and *stay there.* They go to the same place every summer (I don't object to that, except that I would like to go to Europe sometime), and then in the

Spring, when they might take trips around to different places to see something of the country, they go to the same place. I, for one, am tired of Atlantic City. The kid only says "Go to Atlantic City" because she knows nothing else. I would prefer some other place, say Old Point Comfort.

Mammy dear you really don't half read my letters. I *suggested* going by boat, how about it?

And, Mother, *all thought of myself aside,* Daddy *ought* to go away for two weeks. When Cousin Robert was up here last, he agreed with me that being President of the Piano Co. was wearing, and that if Daddy only thought so, he could stay away from business for that long. If the doctor ordered him to he would have to. Do talk to Dad about it.

We have had to fill up the place at our table vacated by Clara. A Freshman now sits with us, but it was so much better before.

Love to the family,<br>Fan

---

March 23

Dearest Dad,

As I wrote Mother, I would prefer Old Point. And Daddy, just let your business go (and we'll all do without summer clothes) and stay two weeks.

Dad, we are going to have two plays up here. One of them is named *A Proposal Under Difficulties*. It is in the June 1895 number of Harpers Monthly Magazine. The other is called, *The Fatal Message,* and is in the February 1896 number of the same magazine. If you can find these two numbers at home, would you mind sending them to me *at once*. I'll take good care of them and bring them home Easter. Send them either in the bound or paper edition.

Yours with love,<br>Fan

Dearest Mother,

I am very glad that the matter of our trip is decided, and I am delighted that we are to go to Old Point Comfort.

By the way, Mother, I am very anxious for a gray felt Knox walking hat, to wear with my gray suit and other things. Mary is delighted to go with us. I got a letter from her yesterday. She said that her mother was just recovering from the grippe, but that her Aunt Maria de Camp was coming to Albany to stay with Mrs. Banks, so that Mary could leave all right.

The McCurdys are here, and it's simply great to have them. The play was a grand success.

Must check my rapid flow of words and bid you adieu.

As ever yours,
Fan

---

April 15

Dearest Mother,

Arrived safely, Lots of girls on train. Must go recite.
Yours,
Fan

---

In class at Vassar
April 16

Mother mine,

I am now in the geology classroom. We have just had a written lesson on Paleontology and as I have written all I know about what he asked us, I thought I'd write you a letter.

We are not going to draw for rooms until tomorrow night. They keep putting the evil hour off. I wish it was all over and I had a room near all the rest of the girls.

We have hired a yacht for the 27th from Dr. Miller, the

dentist. I believe it is a very good one, and he is going to give it to us for $25. Isn't that pleasant?

Yours,

Fan

P.S.  Mother, I drew 31 which is not at all bad (total number 118) We choose this morning.

---

April 19

Dearest Mother,

I got a dear little peanut of a room on the 3rd floor. It is about 2 x 4, but it has two windows, a south one and a west one. It has to be redecorated. Mabel Day is right under me. I really think that I was very fortunate. And Oh! it has a closet, which is more than a lot of the Main singles have.

Am off to the dentist.

Your,

Fan

---

April 21

Dearest Dad my dear,

The box of fruit was the finest I ever saw. I just love everything in it. We have all been eating ever since it arrived, and there's nothing to equal it, *Nothing!*

Daddy mine you are a love. Write soon to

Fanny-who-loves-you

---

April 21

Dearest Mother,

It is a rainy Sunday afternoon, which is really a blessing once in a while. I have so many little things to finish up, in the way of letter-writing, lessons, special topics etc.

First, about Founders: I'll need my slippers (the ones you put the buckles on). Fred is coming. Also Emery, if there is not a Glee Club Concert that day, at Princeton. Friday night is the dance here, and Saturday morning our Glee

Club Concert. Then we send the men down town for lunch and meet them at the boat at three o'clock. The boat is a perfectly safe one and I won't need my fur cape, as we have plenty of coats, golf capes, sweaters, etc.

Yesterday afternoon there was a Qui Vive debate. Nina was on it and really did very well, considering that she hardly worked on it at all. After the debate Omega gave a play. Maude was the villain, Baron Von Snooks; she was splendid. The play was a funny one called, *The Baron's Victim* by Tudor Jenks.

This morning a Mr. McDowell of New York preached. He was pretty good. We had the pineapple cut up with sugar on it and it was simply delicious.

My room for next year has awful looking paper on it and horrid carpet. Guess I'll have new paper and have the carpet taken up and use rugs. That's much cleaner anyway. Mabel Day is right below me, Nina is across the hall, Helen Crosby just around the corner and Florence Dunning above.

Maude, Helen Crum, Gertrude, Grace and Frances are all up on 5th center, each in a single facing South. We had a great time on Friday deciding about rooms. They wanted me and Nina to come up on 5th center with them, but I thought best to stay where I was. I'll explain all about it when I see you.

Guess I'll study a bit. With much love, yours as ever,
Fan

---

Mother mine, excuse paper, but I didn't want to waste it. Mercy me, you don't seem to understand about rooms in Main at all.

In the first place, we all talked it over and decided that singles were the best for us all to choose (in prefence to parlors with corridor bedrooms or *awful* doubles of which there are only a few). Now on the corridors which run from the elevator in each direction are only parlors with corridor bed-rooms. *Almost all* the singles are in the two wings or else on 1st or 5th floors. By the time it got to choice 31, all the singles on 2nd and 3rd south wing were gone. (There are not as many in that wing as in the North, on account of the pro-fessors' suites). So I had to choose in the North wing, or else a bit of a room facing North, or else on 1st, poor rooms on 4th or 5th. So I was very lucky to get a corner room on 3rd, facing southwest. Would you rather have had me choose a bit of a room in 5th center with only one window?

Your,

Fan

---

April 24

Dearest Mother,

You make me *perfectly weary* about my room! I have one of the *best* rooms in Main. La! What do you expect? A corner room with 2 windows, one south and one west, is considered a *great luxury* up here. And none of the singles are any bigger than a peanut. My! you ought to see some of the other girls' rooms. Nina's, for instance, which has a single window facing north, not a bit of sun all day long. And my room will be just flooded with sun-shine. Maude's is a little room on the 5th, with a single narrow window. And think of mine, a corner room, south-west, on third floor, plenty of room to turn around in and a *closet*. Lots of the singles and all the parlor rooms have just wardrobes, and the wardrobes of the singles are all out in the corridor. Think of that! Mercy me!

The kid will be tickled to death with the pony cart, won't she? Who is to drive it? I should think William would break it down.

Yours devotedly,

Fan

123

Mother mine,

I am furious. Emery wrote that he could not come to Founders. I telegraphed Will Howe and he has not yet answered. If he does not come I will be without a man. Oh! these men, these men! I hate 'em all.

Hall Play is to be on the 11th. I want Helen Halsey and you to come up for it. If I can get another guest seat, I want Aunt Esther too.

Will it ever stop raining?

Yours with love,
Fan

---

April 26

Dearest Mother,

I am awfully sorry to have been so cross about my room. But we really had quite a fuss choosing, so I suppose that is what makes me so touchy about it.

Mammy mine, I am all upset about my plans. Will has refused, says he cannot possibly get off. So Fred is the only one coming. Maude was to take him, but now says that of course I must take him, and she'll go alone. I don't want to do that, but what can I do? It is a great temptation to me to write Fred that I can't be here after all, but that if he wants to come, Maude will take care of him. You see it is a holiday tomorrow, so I could come home today and stay until Sunday. But the girls say that it would be a "dirty mean trick" if I go, so I suppose I'll stay up here. You see they've counted me in for the boat ride, etc.

Oh! Mammy, I don't know what to do. I simply *cannot* plan. I wish I had you here to talk to. Could you think of any man I could ask to come up tomorrow? But of course there isn't any near enough, whom I would care to ask that way.

La! me! what a muddle things are, to be sure. 7 weeks and I'll be a *Senior*.

Yours with love,
Fan

---

April 29

My dearest Mammy,

It was most successful. How did you ever get Will to come? I want to thank you for the cakes. When I got your letter I went over and telephoned down to the express office at the station and told them to keep my package there and I would call for it about three o'clock. So I stopped off on my way to the boat and got it. They all sent thanks to you for it, especially Prof. French, our chaperone. He ate *six* at least.

Fred arrived all right for the dance, and was just as nice as ever. He sent Maude some violets and me some candy.

Will came up about half past twelve and I took him around the campus a while, before the boat ride. The men went back on the 9.53. And I think that they enjoyed themselves ever so much. They seemed to.

Weren't we lucky in our weather?

Devotedly,
Fan

---

Last day of April, 1901

Dearest Mother,

The weather! Oh it is hot, and I don't have a thin thing to wear. I need low shoes like the dickens. And can't you send me my pink and white mercerized cotton sailor suits? If they need washing, I'll have them done here. Also my white dotted swiss and one of my plain white low-neckers. I really ought to go home this week to shop.

Yours,
Fan

May 1

Dearest Mother,

Went to the Able General's office this noon and got permission (without much fuss) to go to New York May 3-5. So I'll be at Grand Central at 2.55 on Friday.

Of course you can have my gray hat. Only too glad to get rid of it.

Yours with love,
Fan

---

Monday 8 A.M.

Dearest Mother,

Arrived safely; one instructor and two or three girls on the train. Maude, Nina, Grace, Gertrude and Frances walked 22 miles yesterday, and they are really limping around today. Have to go.

Yours,
Fan

---

May 8

Dearest Mother,

I am looking forward so much to having all you people up here for the Hall Play. Maude and I will meet you at the station on Saturday at 10.31.

Match game with the sophs this afternoon at 4. I am not going to play, as I have not been able to practice during the past week, but I'm going out in my gym suit, in case I'm needed.

Poor old Maude is laid up with blisters on her feet from the long walk on Sunday. Love to the household,

Fan

---

May 9

Mother mine,

Took poor old Maudie over to the infirmary last night

with the same thing the matter with her she had up at the Lake. Hope she'll be out by Saturday.

Hurrah we beat the Sophomores 6 to 0. Isn't that great? Bully for 1902. This is my busy day.

Your<br>Fan

---

4 P.M. May 14

Mother mine,

Maude is no worse and not much better. Fever and pulse about the same. Dr. Thelberg is telephoning Dr. M. her exact condition, and for him to decide about the operation.

Love to Dad and the kid.

Lovingly,<br>Fan

---

May 15

Mother mine,

Maude is the same. I still spend quite a good deal of time with the doctor, as I would rather learn Maude's condition from her than from Mrs. Wright, as the latter does not seem to know much about sickness, even if the patient is her own daughter. She wanted to get Maude some strawberries yesterday, for instance. Mrs. Wright is still staying in the room and she is very appreciative of all we girls do.

Yours with love,<br>Fan

---

May 20

Dearest Mother,

This morning immediately after breakfast I went over to see Dr. Thelberg. She said that she had not yet told Mrs. Wright, but that Dr. Marco had decided that an operation was necessary. The inflammation has all centered in one spot and they think there is an abcess formed there. Dr. Marco is to charge $500, but don't mention that.

Oh! Mother the operation must be successful, and Maude must get well. I am going over some time before dinner and find out when Dr. M. is coming. Am now going out for a little airing.

With love, yours,<br>Fan

---

8 P.M. May 21

Dearest Mother,

*I have been in to see Maude.* I went up to the Doctor's room to see how Maude was. Dr. M. is coming up tomorrow to perform the operation (if he thinks it necessary which he probably will).

Then Dr. Thelberg said, "Fanny, would you like to see Maude for a minute or two?" Mother, just think of it. And I went in and talked to her for a whole minute! She was just grand, said she was so glad to see me. I'm the only visitor she's had. I just smiled at her and she smiled at me and she talked so cheerfully, showed me the icewater coils, said Dr. Marco had been up and was coming again either today or tomorrow, said she had something the matter with her side. (She doesn't know it's appendicitis)

Mammy, she's got to pull through tomorrow all right.

Good-night, dear. I'm *so* glad I saw her.

Your Fan

---

May 24

Mother Mine,

We play the Seniors this afternoon. Just think, if we only beat them we have the championship. But Oh! gee! I'm so afraid we won't.

Saw Maude's nurse this morning. The nurse Dr. Marco brought with him was taken ill. So Maude has the one she had before the operation. I then went over to see Dr. Thelberg (as I always think I get a truer statement of the case from her), but she wasn't home, so I'll go see her again this afternoon.

Helen Crum sails on June 8th (Hamburg-American). The girls are thinking of going down to see her off. What about having them stop at the house Friday night, the 7th. I'd like to have Grace and Gertrude for over that Sunday too.

I am having a time deciding what to elect for next year. We have 12 hours a week Senior year. Ethics (3 hours) is required. So I have 9 more hours to elect. I have fully decided to take F. Economics (3 hours). Then I have 6 hours left to decide upon. The ones among which I think of choosing are: C. Art (3 hours), B. German (3 hours), J. Greek (3 hours), and A. Physiology (3 hours).

If I dropped both Greek and German, I would not have anything at all on Friday. That would certainly be good, but I rather hate to drop all languages. I am going to talk to Miss McCurdy before I decide.

We had the grandest time with Cousin Robert yesterday, Mabel, Nina, Grace, Gertrude and I.

Only two more weeks of it !

Yours with love,<br>Fan

---

May 25

Dearest Mother,

Isn't it perfectly terrible the way those awful things have come out in the papers? I do think that it is criminal to publish such stuff. How do you suppose it got in the papers? And there's just enough truth in them to make it awful ! Poor little Maude, to be so slandered, and she never even thought of reducing her weight when she took that long walk!

She had a very good night last night. I saw the doctor this morning and she said that Maude was getting along all right from the operation, but she thinks that the appendicitis isn't over yet. I guess she'll have to have another operation in a week or two.

Helen and Frances are in New York today. Nasty day for them. And also for the college settlement children who are here today.

Yours with love,
Fan

---

May 27

Dearest Mother,

Why under the shining stars did Mrs. Reilly send my two new dresses up here? Well, I'll try them on and bring them home with me next week. Thank you for the box of food. After I had unpacked the box and thrown away the paper, I was sitting reading and happened to look down and saw two $10 bills on the floor. Did you send them in the box you sent me? Thank you muchly if you did, but I might easily have thrown them away.

Lovingly,
Fan

---

May 27 — later

Mother dearest,

I am wildly crazy to get home. I was never so tired of college in my life.

I thought when Mrs. Wright came, I would have done with responsibility, but alas not so. In the first place, Mrs. Wright looks tired out, and I'm afraid she'll break down. And then — Maude has just one nurse, so while she (the nurse) has her rest in the afternoon, Mrs. Wright takes care of Maude. The back legs of Maude's bed are propped up, so that Maude lies on a slant. There is a tube in the abscess, so they won't let Maude sit up yet. Mrs. Wright told me a day or two ago that Maude had written a note home. She said, "The nurse would never have let her, if she had known it". Then last night Mrs.

130

Wright brought over a 3 page note from Maude for us girls. She told Mabel the same thing, that the nurse would never have let her.

And yet Mrs. Wright keeps telling people how much she knows about sickness. Goodness knows whether she lets Maude do anything else when she's with her. Mrs. Wright said that Maude couldn't sit up, because they were afraid the tube might slip. Now shouldn't you think it would be quite a strain for her to write? Oh! it is absolutely incomprehensible to me. And I think that I ought to tell the Doctor about the note we got, because if the Doctor doesn't want Maude to write, why I'd never forgive myself if anything should come of it.

My! Mother, it's hard to decide what one ought to do in a case like this. You see writing may not do her any harm at all.

On Friday we beat the Seniors 4-2. Hurrah for 1902. Last night the Juniors gave the Seniors a boat ride. It was great fun.

All this week is review, review, review.

Yours with love,<br>Fan

P.S. *Please* destroy this letter. I don't want any details of M's illness in existence.

---

May 28

My poor dear little Mother,

I am so sorry to hear that you have been ill, and hope that you are all right again now, dear.

Last night I had a long talk with the doctor. She said the abscess was all healed up but Maude has a fever and maybe another is forming, or else that her appendix itself is the trouble.

The college is crazy about those *awful* newspaper reports. Prexy talked about it last night in chapel and said the girls had no right to let any newspaper man get hold of anything about the college. They are rampant. So, for goodness sake,

131

don't mention anything I tell you *to a soul*. The very walls have ears. There was an account in *The Chicago Tribune* with a real picture of Maude. The account of her walk and illness has gone from New York to San Francisco.

Mr. Wright wrote us the sweetest letter thanking us for what we've done. He also said that they were greatly relieved that Maude was on the road to a speedy recovery. Oh! law!

I think Dr. Thelberg is very anxious to have her taken to St. Luke's in New York, as she is crazy with all the responsibility. And if there were another operation, Dr. Marco ought to be the one to take care of Maude, and he can't come up to Po'keepsie every day to dress the wound. And the college closes next week.

Don't breathe this to anybody. Dr. T. said she had not told a soul how she felt about the responsibility.

Well, Mammy, hope you'll be all right now. Love to Dad and the kid. Tear up this letter!

Yours with love,
Fan

---

May 29

Dearest Dad,

My! I was glad to get your letter this morning. I breathed again. I am so glad that we can find out Maude's condition from Dr. Spaulding. He will know, won't he? Because I really would like to know more than Mrs. Wright could tell me. I am so glad you and Mother are in New York to be nice to Mrs. Wright and Maude.

3 dozen roses came here for her from Fred today. Wasn't that pleasant of him?

I do hope Mammy is better. I'm now going to pack up all Maude's things, leaving here the things she'll want next year and sending her trunk down to St. Luke's.

You were a love to go to the station and meet Maude. Love to Mother and the kid.

Yours,

Fan

---

Dearest Mother,

I was so glad to get your letter saying that the operation was successful. Mother Flett went down with Mrs. Wright, and stayed until last night. Mother Flett I saw this morning. She said that they had removed the appendix. Can't you find out the particulars of the operation from Dr. Spaulding? Was there another abscess? Dr. Spaulding is a dear. I am so glad he is connected with St. Luke's. Of course he'd be crazy about Maude if he ever met her. She is a pippin!

Now, about the kid and her school. As far as that note of Miss Spence's goes, a child changing schools *never* fits in to her new class very ideally. All schools run their classes on different plans. When I changed to Miss Brown's I did not fit ideally into any of her classes. I don't believe the kid would fit in much better after another year at Miss Schoonmaker's than she does now.

I don't know quite what to tell you, but it seems to me that if you intend changing the kid's school at all, it would be better to do it right away. Then next year, she could get fitted into a class at Miss Spence's far better by being there, than by continuing her work at Miss Schoonmaker's. As for the kid not wanting to go, of course she doesn't; she'd be a mighty strange child if she did. But she would soon get acquainted with children at Miss Spence's, and probably get to know some who live near "988." That would be so much less lonesome for her.

Luncheon

After a delicious lunch of ham and bread and sugar, I

133

take my pen in hand again. Now, Mammy, do whatever you think best about the kid.

Where on earth do you suppose those two ten dollar bills came from? They must have been in the box you sent me, as there were only two girls in the room that afternoon, and neither of them had that much money. Think hard if there was any possible way they could have fallen in.

Yours with love,
Fan

---

June 1

Mother mine,

I guess if I don't let you know to the contrary, I'll take the 4.50 train from here on Thursday, wearing my blue silk dress and black hat and taking my blue coat, arriving at Peekskill at 5.47. Then you and Dad (if he decides to go to the wedding) wait at the Peekskill station for me, bringing me a pair of white gloves, and we'll all go to the church together. Please be sure to wait for me, because I'll be scared by myself.

It seems to me that you must have had an unusually hard attack last Sunday for the effects to last so long. I am worried about you, Mother.

I am on the committee for the Senior Parlor. I won't do a thing but raid both Nirvana* and "988."

Some of the girls are coming down on Friday. We are going to see Helen Crum off Saturday. (Ask Dad to get courtesies of the port if necessary). And then Grace, Gertrude, Nina and perhaps Mabel, will stay with us until Monday, when we all come back up here for class day.

Guess I'll cram.

Yours with love,
Fan

* *Nirvana was the name of the Simpson's summer home at Lake George.*

134

Dearest Mother,

Well, dear, this is my busy week. I hear that the exam papers are to be *unusually hard* this year, because they are to be sent to the Pan American Exposition. Pleasant prospect, isn't it? and as I have had so much on my mind for the past month and consequently have not done much studying, why don't be surprised if I flunk.

Well, I'll to my Greek. Love to Dad and the kid.

your<br>Fan

---

June 5

Dearest my Mother,

Why don't you answer what I ask you? You have never mentioned our going down to see Helen off and have not said that you would meet me in Peekskill with my white gloves, and please dear read my letters more carefully. I asked you if you could find out the particulars of Maude's operation.

Mammy, I asked you if you would please ask Dad to get the courtesies of the port for us to see Helen off. She sails on the Patricia I think it's on the Holland-American line, but I'm not sure.

Then, Mammy, we girls are of course very anxious to see Maude, and I believe it is necessary to get permission from the Doctors. Now they might not let so many people in to see her in one day. I would like to go see her Friday morning (after I've been to the milliners), but if it is going to prevent other girls from seeing her that afternoon, I won't go in until Saturday. Mammy, will you please ask Dr. Spaulding to get permission for Helen Crum, Mrs. Crum and Frances Fenton to see her on Friday. Then on Saturday the rest of us could see her, or on Sunday or Monday. Mammy dear, will you please get this permission, please, because they might be particular about letting the girls go in, and Helen is very anxious to see her before she sails. I suppose if you asked Dr. Spaulding and he left word at the hospital the names of the girls, who were to be let in to see Maude, they would get in without any trouble.

Yours with love,
Fan

---

Dearest Mother,

My train was an hour late, but I tell you, I am getting to be a seasoned traveller. There was a bride and groom across the aisle from me. They were both wearing patent leather shoes to travel in. Sure sign! She talks continually of "Mamma." Another b. and g. had their heads on the same pillow. On my other side were three old men, none under 70. It was an interesting car full.

Am having a perfect time. The dress from McCreery and waist from Briggs came. The ball is going to be the finest thing of its kind ever given here. The house-party has not turned out very well, as there are only four of us, counting Ethel (Dave is not home). But it does not matter, as there are some town men here all the time, and three or four are to sit in our box tonight.

Must say farewell.

Yours with love,
Fan

# THE GROUP

*turn of the century*

## SENIOR YEAR

September 23, 1901

Dearest Mother,

We had a good trip down from Lake George, though I never saw so many invalids as there were in our car. A woman dying of consumption sat right across the aisle, and six or seven people (all with something awful the matter with them), got on at Saratoga. I think they must have been from some sanitarium. When we got off the train at Poughkeepsie, who should be there but Gertrude, Grace and Maude! They had come to meet us. Wasn't that pleasant of them? They suggested going right to Smiths for dinner, which we did.

My room is fine! I just love the wallpaper. The matting is here and I'm going to have it put on tomorrow. I'm also going shopping tomorrow for my desk, bookcase, and chair. Please send me the mahogany dresser out of the yellow room right away. I measured the space and it's plenty big enough.

Gertrude Barnard, who is on the committee with me for Senior Parlor, says they have not done a thing about it yet, so I'm awfully glad that I stayed at the Lake. You know the committee has to furnish this whole large parlor, each year, and then we have a big opening with the Glee Club singing etc.

Mother it is all simply great to be back here. I just love it! Helen Crum came back last night. I was so glad to see her. She's just the same old girl. Brought me a pair of gloves from Paris.

My room is very bright, sunny, airy and nice.

Love to all, especially Dad and the kid.

Yours,

Fan

---

September 27

Dearest Mother,

Received two letters from you this morning, one special delivery. Am glad that you are going to send the dresser as I am anxious to get settled. My curtains will have to wait until you get home. Just think, my white curtains (to hang from inside window to floor), will have to be 11 feet long, and my silk curtains a few inches longer. Did you ever hear of such long windows?

Mammy will you please see if you can find my glasses and send them to me. I have my smoked ones, but I want the others.

Mother, I don't know quite why you suggest sending me four rugs. Do you mean for my room or the Senior Parlor? I think the two fur rugs would be very nice in my room, so please send those.

I am through my work Fridays at 9.20 A.M. Will you please send *one* of those oak chairs which are in the hall. You

know, the ones with the carved backs. We need it for Senior
Parlor.

Lovingly,<br>Fan

---

7 A.M. September 28

PERSONAL

Dearest Mother,

This morning I woke up early and got so nervous thinking
about Dad, that I'm going to write a letter. How is he? You
don't suppose anything is *really* the matter with him. His terrible headaches have not affected his head? Please write and
tell me that he is his old self. I'm silly, but don't you care.

Bell has just rung. Love to Dad and the kid. Tell them to
write to me.

Yours,<br>Fan

---

September 28

Dear Little Kid,

Please send me a hair-receiver, rather large, because my
hair is coming out by the bushel. Something in sweet grass or
birch bark.

This morning I fussed around my room, doing carpentry
work. This afternoon shopped. Bought some peaches, and
Nina bought some grapes, so I guess I'll go eat.

Yours with love,<br>Titter

---

October 2

Dearest Mother,

Maude and I will leave here Friday getting to Grand
Central at 1.30. We'll go to the Plaza for lunch. Gertrude and
Clara will be down later. Fred wants us to go to the theatre

with him. I hope the girls won't feel uncomfortable visiting us at a hotel. Well I must write Fred and then do Greek.

Yours with love,<br>Fan

---

October 10

Dearest Mother,

Mrs. K. called Maude and me up, but we were so surprised — she did not make any fuss at all; just said that we must not do it again, without telegraphing or writing to college for permission. And then of course only if it was very important.

The way she found it out was this. There was some mistake about the room for Phil. meeting, so she looked up the President and the Vice-President, and found them both in New York. It turned out all right. Must go to a recitation.

Lovingly,<br>Fan

---

October 11

Dearest Mother,

We initiate the new members into Shakespeare tonight. Expect to have an awfully jolly time.

Mother I was never so flabbergasted as when I heard about Frances Warren. Isn't it dreadful? Why she's hardly over typhoid yet, and Hope only born a year ago, and now another one. Gee!

The decorator from Tiffany's is here about the Senior Parlor, and we are all very much excited. I am glad you and Dad had such a good time on your trip. How is Dad? How is the kid getting along at School?

I am so very busy now, it seems as if I didn't have a moment. What with Senior Parlor, arranging for Shakespeare Club initiation, and innumerable meetings such as representative, Phil., Students, etc. Gee! as I said before.

Don't worry about Mrs. K. having called me up. She didn't seem to mind at all.

Yours with love,<br>Fan

---

October 13

Dearest Mother,

We had the most perfect day yesterday you can possibly imagine. Seventeen girls, Dr. and Mrs. Mills, Dr. Moore, Mrs. K, Miss Ely and a friend of hers composed the party. We left the dock at 11 o'clock, and had a beautiful sail down the river as far as West Point, having lunch on the boat. The yacht we had belongs to Dr. Miller, the dentist. It is 85 feet long and perfectly equipped. Has the cutest little cabin and stateroom for eight people, and the whole upper deck is covered with an awning. At West Point we landed and went up to see the West Point-Trinity football game. Grace Bruce's brother is a sub on the Trinity team. It seemed so queer to be at the Point and not know any of the cadets. I felt quite homesick for '98, '99, 1900 and 1901. We left the Point at quarter of five and sailed back home again, having a light supper on board. At 7.30 we got back to college, and found that Mrs. K. had ordered supper saved for us. In the evening Christian Association gave a party to the Freshmen. Also tableaux and refreshments.

I am glad the kid likes her new school. It is so nice for her to meet children, who live somewhere in the neighborhood.

Love to Dad and the kid,

Yours,<br>Fan

---

October 14

Dearest Mother,

Measured the space in Senior Parlor for the sheep picture and find that it is just right. We are all tickled to death about it.

On Saturday we go to Mohonk, weather permitting.

141

Maude is getting along very nicely. She passed off her last exam on Friday, so now she is even with the class once more.

The campus is beautiful right now. I wish that you could see it.

As regards the parlor. We can't decide whether to have the opening on the 2nd or the 9th. We are crazy to have it on the 2nd, that is the customary day to have it, and the sooner the parlor is open the better. As far as work goes, the longer we have the longer we'll take. The only question is whether the furniture will all be here in time. The decorator is to be through this week. Then the floor has to be done, and the furniture put in and arranged. Our pictures and rugs we can get here in time. In fact most of them are here now. The serious question is this. Flint and Vetter *swore* that they would ship furniture on the 28th by boat, *asserting* that it would *positively* get here on the next day. Now if they don't keep their word, of course we are in a hole.

There are two or three things which have to be done *at once*. So Gertrude and I will be down on *Wednesday* (day after tomorrow) on the 1.05 train. The three things we have to do are: (1) see the piano, (2) look at shades in 125th St. and (3) buy a desk.

Clara went to Donnell's and he said he would make up some shades. ($30 for 14). Clara liked the design very much, but the trouble is that they are lower than the sample and the mantle or chimney or something (he did not make himself very clear) would show over the top. If the ones in 125th St. are pretty and have not that defect, we would rather have them. Gertrude and I will want address of 125th St. store and sample globe. Lighting is surely a problem.

In regard to the desk, the girl who was to buy a desk at Flints, does not like it and won't buy it. So we have countermanded that order. Another girl will give a desk for about $40 to $50. Clara saw a desk at Manby's (1 West 38th St.) for $45.

It was a bit smaller than the one at Flint's, but the right kind of wood, so that it would not have to be done over. She was not wildly enthusiastic about it, but if Gertrude and I see nothing we like better and *it is not sold,* we are going to get it.

I guess the best plan would be for us to get off at 125th St., and go to factory and shade store, and then down town. *Could you* meet us somewhere? We come back on the 6.25 train.

Must go to art. Hope you can make something out of this long letter. Hope the kid is better. Helen Crosby is in the infirmary.

Love to Dad,<br>
Your Fan

---

October 17

Dearest Mother,

We got back last night quite satisfied with our day's work. But alas! the girls did not like the shades, so Clara is going down tomorrow to see what she can do.

The man has all the frieze beneath the moulding finished and is now at work obliterating last year's frieze.

Helen Crosby got out of the infirmary today.

I must write Ethel that I hope to see her on her way back from the bicentennial.

Will see you at Mohonk Saturday.

Yours,<br>
Fan

---

October 29

Dearest Dad,

Do you think you could get the Schenck sheep picture off on Wednesday (tomorrow)? If not then, please get it off on Thursday without fail. We want Mr. Baker to come on Friday to hang pictures.

The great big rug which Nina Eldred is to give is not

143

panning out very well. She wants to rent one. Have you any idea where we could rent a rug? The space to be covered is 25 feet by 8 feet 9 inches, but of course it would be most difficult to get a rug very near those dimensions. If we could get one somewhere near that width, we could put another rug with it to make up for the length.

Have you a pull at any place where we could rent a rug?

Clara is going down tomorrow on the 1.05 to see about it, and I may have to go with her. So if you know of any place, won't you please telegraph.

Hope the kid is better. Give her my love.

Your,
Fan

---

October 31

Dearest Mother,

Got my annual invitation from Charlie for the New Years dance in Roselle, or any of the informal ones. Ah! the ever faithful!

Yesterday we went to Van G's and Sloane's, finding nothing. The rugs you saw at Sloane's are not pretty, and color won't do at all. Lucy Burns told us her father had a pull at Kostikyan's. She did not know the address. We asked at the different rug stores and they told us there were two Kostikyans, one "Kostikyan Freres", and one "Kent and Kostikyan". We found Kent and Kostikyan right opposite Sloane's on the 6th floor. So up we went, marched in and asked for Oriental Rugs. We saw just what we wanted, a beautiful Iran rug, 16 feet by 7 feet (or something like that), just the right colors, sort of brown and blue with a yellowish border, small pattern etc. We asked how much it was and the man said $120. We gasped at its being so cheap. (We had seen nothing approaching it for less than 300 or 400). The man said something about that being wholesale, and asked who sent us. We gasped and said "Mr. Burns", not knowing whether we were in the right store or not. He said, "Oh yes, I was told that Mr. Burns was going to send someone in here". At that we were so relieved. Imagine us walking into a wholesale place!

The man said he might make some arrangements about renting it to us for the year. He was to speak to Mr. Kostikyan and wire us this morning. We have not heard yet. Nina Eldred said that she would rent it for a month and then buy it out of her own allowance. So we are all anxiously awaiting the telegram. Don't you want to pay half and then one or the other of us buy the other one out in June? Nina, I am sure, would be willing to buy it, cause she said she would.

That is of course if they refuse to rent it.

The number of the rug is (I can't find it). It's in Clara Russell's name, if you want to look at it.

Well, so long.

Yours,

Fan

Later: we are so worried about not getting the telegram, and we ought to have the rug right away. Can't you go in there tomorrow morning and tell them to send the rug *immediately by express*. Can't you give references so that they will send the bill instead of sending it C.O.D. It really ought to be here on Saturday. Enclosed is card with No. of rug.

---

November 2

Dearest Dad,

The picture came yesterday. Mr. Baker with the aid of Mr. Downing, another man, Gertrude and myself, got it up safely and secured. It is hung by heavy wire on two heavy iron hooks, and rests on two iron hooks. It is simply *perfect*. Thanks, thanks, thanks!

Enclosed find bill for papering my room here. Must go to Qui Vive meeting.

Yours,

Fan

Dearest Mother,

Have just written to Cousin Robert and Ella to come up for the opening of Senior Parlor next Saturday. I have secured five seats at the guest table, so you can all come up to college for dinner that night at six o'clock.

Last night we gave a Halloween party to the sophomores on the Senior Corridor. We fixed the corridor and rooms off it as the midway at the Pan. It was really quite the funniest thing I've ever been to.

Will you ask Dad to send me a translation of Plato's Republic. I would rather have Jowett's translation, but if Hinds and Noble have not that, why, any one will do. Don't have them mail it from the store.

Yours with love,<br>Fan

---

Estey Piano Co.<br>New York City<br>November 4

My dear Fanny

The piano stool will be shipped from here tomorrow by boat, and reach Poughkeepsie about 9 P.M., so there seems to be no apparent reason why it should not be delivered Wednesday morning. I have requested Mr. Vossler to inform you by mail or telephone just when it will be delivered.

Your invitation for next Saturday is certainly appreciated. To be invited to meet the intelligence, beauty and strong womanly characters of Vassar College, that is largely represented in the class of 1902, is an honor not to be considered in a light manner. As to my acceptance, I shall have to confer with Ella and let you know later. I feel somewhat like making it a condition of my being present, that I'm permitted to sing a solo subject "Darling Mabel, do you love me?" with Miss Mabel Day at the piano, or that other popular song, "What has become of Nina's rum?" with Miss Nina Blackmer at the piano. I might be satisfied with giving a recitation, subject, "Did you ever see Maude eat macaroons?"

Sincerely,
Your Cousin Robert

---

November 6

Mother mine,

What with the Senior Parlor and playing sick nurse to Nina, mine has been a busy life for the last few days. The college seems to have suddenly fallen ill. There are 31 seniors ill and about the same number in other classes. Prexy says there have never been so many ill since he was President. Mumps and tonsilitis are the principal afflictions. *Don't* say anything about so many girls being ill, as it could make quite a newspaper story.

The light globes came, and are right pretty. I was pleasantly surprised, but am not crazy about them.

Mammy will you please get some nice baby things this week, and send them to Frances from me.

Your,
Fan

---

November 10

Dearest Mother,

It was just grand to have you and Dad and Cousin Robert here for the Opening.

Brinton Buckwalter wants to know if he can call on me Sunday (the 17th) in New York. Isn't it funny I'll just happen to be there?

Goodnight, dear.

---

November 13

Dearest Mother,

Maude, Nina and I will take the 1.05 train down on Friday. It is Maude's 21st birthday Friday the 15th, so let's have

147

a grand celebration that night. Can't we have a birthday cake with 21 candles? Please have the cake itself good. Can't you get a chocolate clear through with white icing at the Woman's Exchange? And some flowers?

Mrs. K. just gave me permission, but says of course that I can't go again until Xmas. I just looked pleasant, but she'll see!

Am going to town tonight to hear Bertha Galland in *The Forest Lovers.*

Yours,
Fan

---

November 18

Dearest Dad,

When we got to the station, who should appear but Jim Davis. I never saw anything funnier. Nina and Ted were cavorting along, having the best kind of a time, when Jim popped up. He came all the way to Poughkeepsie, going to Meriden by way of Albany.

I don't believe I can possibly come back here next year as a grad. student. I want to be with you and Mother and show you what a nice daughter I can be. I don't know why I was so peevish yesterday. But I love you *hard* just the same and lie awake nights worrying about you when you cough or are despondent. Never mind, I'll be home next year to cheer you up.

Thank you so much for the theatre party. I enjoyed it so much.

Yours with love,
Fan

---

November 19

Dearest Mother,

I left my two new Hannis and Jenkins stocks at home. One

is blond satin, and the other black silk with white stitching. Would you mind sending them to me.

My special topic for Economics is "Children's Courts." Would you mind sending me right away the Tribune for Sunday, Nov. 17th. I believe there is an item on the subject in it.

The National Conference of Charities and Correction is held in New York during this week. On Thursday night there is to be a paper on Juvenile Courts. If you see anything in the paper about it, just cut it out, will you? Anybody is welcome at the conference, so as I get a cut from Greek on Friday, I *may* suddenly take it into my head to come down for it, but I don't believe I will.

Must go to lunch,

Fan

---

November 20

I know, dear little Mammy, how busy you are this week with your Church Fair, and I hate to bother you, but we are tickled to death about the cheesecloth. So could about 400 yards of white be sent the minute the fair is over, (the cleanest white that there is, of course)? And could you send me samples of green and directions as to place of getting it and price, right away. You see the cheesecloth has to be made up into little dew-dads for decoration before it is put up.

I told Caroline last night that I can't be chairman of the Intercollegiate Debate. I just hated to do it, but I've thought and thought and that seems the only thing to do.

Could you send me a box of food to get here Saturday? I think I'll cook breakfast in the room Sunday morning, so if you could send me some partridge or chicken, a bit of coffee (ready ground), I'll be deeply grateful.

Yours with love,
Fan

December 1

Dearest Mother,

My last Phil. dance is over! And my it was fun! I enjoyed every minute of it. Will and Ted were dandy. Thank Dad a thousand times for the set of favors. He is a *love*.

The kid and Don are certainly "going it," are they not?

Goodnight, Mammy dear,

Yours,

Fan

---

December 4

Dearest Mother,

Have been so busy with the German and being chairman of the Greek play, that I have not had time to write you.

I would like to have Mabel spend Christmas with us. Helen Crum is not going home for vacation. She is going up to Clara Holt's for part of vacation. How about asking her to spend the rest of the time with us, and having a house-party.

Yours,

Fan

---

December 5

Dearest Mother,

Yesterday it snowed hard here so that today there is sleighing. Today has been glorious. I walked for about 2 hours this afternoon.

The favors for the German came and I am very pleased with them. (Thank you, Daddy mine, for going to Schwartz)

Gee! I hope Ethel Boies gives a house-party for the Bachelor's Ball in Scranton. I don't see why she couldn't give it with her mother away. (All the better! Hush! What did I hear you say?)

Your,

Fan

Dearest Mother,

Hurrah! Invitation from Ethel to Scranton Christmas time! Mrs. B. has been ill, so she did not write before. Two other girls and a lot of fellows will be there! Hurrah! I can go, can't I Mammy? Ethel is going to be at the Waldorf Dec. 10-13, Xmas shopping with her mother and father.

Yours,

Fan

---

December 7

Dearest Mother,

Are you very busy, or will you have time to do one or two little errands for me. 1. Will you order me some more visiting cards at Tiffany's? 2. If you happen to be near the 5 and 10 cent store, will you stop in and ask them to put a tracer on the things they sent me by freight last Friday. 3. Then I am going to have a little Xmas tree in the middle of the favor table. Could you send me some of the best looking tree decorations you happen to have? 4. Then do you know where I could get those paper ribbon things, which they threw at the statue at Harvard Class Day? Do you know what I mean? They unwound as they were thrown and hung on the trees in wavy ribbons.

That is all, my dear little Mammy, and I think I'm horrid to ask you to do so much.

Well, dear, this seems to be a letter of requests, so I'll just add one more and stop. Will you ask Dad to please send me some money for Xmas presents.

What do you and Dad and the kid want?

The German is on the evening of the 14th.

---

December 8

Dearest Mother,

Poor little Mammy, you seem quite overwhelmed by the

enthusiastic way I wrote about going to Ethel's. I was so excited with reading her account of the fun we would have, that I was bubbling over. If you and Dad don't want me to go, I'll write her I can't.

Have been busy today making tissue paper muffs for the German. It is 12 degrees below zero here. There is skating, so if you have not sent the box of decorations, would you mind sending my skates with them.

Yours with love,<br>Fan

---

December 9

Dearest Mother,

Got the newspaper clipping about Dad and the faithful footman.* Wasn't it funny?

Mabel's fiancé, Mercer, is here seeing Mabel today. Yesterday Mabel had a letter from Cousin Robert inviting her to come visit them any Sunday she could. She is crazy about going, and is going to write him that she would like to come for the 22nd. You see Xmas vacation is so hard for her, when all the other girls are going home. Mammy dear, I know it is a lot I am asking you, but can't I ask Mabel and Dickie and their fiancés, Mercer and Billy, to dinner on Christmas. You see it won't be a family dinner anyway with Mabel and Dickie there, and Mabel is crazy to have you and Dad meet Mercer and Billy, and they would be *so* happy. It's my last real Christmas vacation, and Mabel and Dick will both be married next year, so please don't think I have a lot of nerve to ask.

Guess Helen Crum will spend all of her vacation with Clara Holt, so I don't have to think about her.

Just a week from Friday, Mammy, and I'll be home. Won't that be pleasant?

---

* *For an account of this incident see page 1*

Mammy, I don't believe I can stand these fur rugs, the hair comes out so. I'll send them home and bring some others back after Xmas.

Your,<br>Fan

---

December 11

Dearest Daddy,

I wish you many happy returns of your birthday! And send you the proper number of kisses.

Thank you very much for the $10. It arrived quite safely.

Mabel and Dickie seem to be so happy about coming to us for Christmas. I am going to write Mercer and Billy to come over in the afternoon, and stay to dinner.

Indeed I am crazy to see Maude Adams in *Quality Street.* Could we work it in sometime while Mabel and Dick are with us. I guess not though, it would probably be too tiresome.

I am going to write Ethel tonight and tell her "yes."

A week from Friday. Think of it.

Yours with love,<br>Fan

---

December 18

Dearest Mother,

To think of Egerton and Stella with an infant! Mother, I feel 150 years old at least! You and Dad say mighty little about the new calendar. It has been the great excitement at college for the past month, and you just pass it by with a "Dad thanks you".

I wrote Charlie Pat. today and refused his kindly offer.

Goodbye until tomorrow at seven.

Your,<br>Fan

153

Scranton, Pa.
December 27

Dearest Mother,

Arrived on time. Ethel was late meeting me, so Max Bessel (who happened to be at the station) put me in a hansom and up I came. Tonight is a dance at the Scrantons', tomorrow night the Assembly. Saturday card party. Monday Ethel is to have some people in, and Tuesday night is the Bachelors. I think this is correct.

Frank Fuller announced his engagement yesterday to a girl named Bertha Powell. Everybody was very much surprised. To think of Frank being engaged! I am certainly going to be a L.O.P.H., (left on Papa's hands), at the rate my friends are going off.

Must get dressed now.

Lovingly,
Fan

---

Scranton, Pa.
December 28

Dearest Mother,

The dance last night was simply perfect. There were lots of men I knew, so it made it very pleasant. Frank and his fiancée were not at the dance last night. Miss Powell is not invited to the small affairs and Frank would not go without her. No more time.

With love,
Fan

---

Scranton, Pa.
December 29

Dearest Mother,

The card party last night was fun, though everybody was sleepy as the dickens.

Mammy, how about my bringing Ethel down to N.Y.

with me on Thursday to stay until Monday. I think that would be the only time she could come until after her trip to Japan. Please write me at once about it.

With love,

Fan

---

Scranton, Pa.

December 30

Dearest Mother,

The dance last night was a bird, no mistake. It was in The Bicycle Clubhouse.

Saw Frank and his fiancée. She is right pretty, but has not a very good carriage.

Tonight we go to a card party, and I must get dressed at once.

With love,

Fan

---

Scranton, Pa.

December 31

Dearest Mother,

We are having the time of our lives.

It would be fun to have a theatre party Friday night with Fred and Arthur (you had better ask them right away), and say, don't tell Arthur that Ethel is coming. How about going to Weber and Fields. We don't mind smoke. Ethel has seen *Monsieur Beaucaire. Message from Mars* is good too, or *The Roger Brothers.*

Am going to Frank Linen's tonight for dinner. Then to the ball.

Yours with love,

Fan

---

January 7, 1902

Dearest Mother,

Would you mind sending me the Sept. 1901 number of

155

the American Journal of Sociology. I guess you can get it at any large bookstore.

We had a class meeting tonight about drawing up resolutions about Emily Loud. Prexy spoke about her death in chapel tonight.

Don't worry about me worrying about my work. It will all come out in the wash.

Am going to write Ethel a bread and butter letter now. Goodnight, Mammy. Much love to Dad.

Fan

---

January 9

Dearest Mother,

Have been working hard today and accomplished quite a good deal, besides going to a tea in honor of the new Biological Laboratory. It is a perfect building, one of the finest we have.

Nothing doing with my vac. as yet. Love to Dad and the kid.

Yours,<br>Fan

---

January 10

Dearest Mother,

Got a letter from Maude. She has had jaundice, catarrh of the stomach and some gland trouble. She's much better and will be back on Saturday.

Am having quite a time with elections for my next semester's work. Have to take 12 hours. The courses I am hesitating between are: K. Greek, M. Greek, B. Physiology, E. Economics, H. Economics and D. Art. I am going to take E. Economics anyway, and as H. Economics is limited to 7 girls, and you have to get permission from the department to take it, and as Dr. Mills said I could, why I guess I'll take it. Besides it's grand, though lots of work, I guess. It's my last chance for any course, so it's hard to choose.

Well, guess I'll read some more criminal stuff. Here's luck.

Fan

---

January 13

Dearest Mother,

These last two have been my busy days. Yesterday from 9.30 to 4.30 on my special topic, and this afternoon I worked on another topic until 4.30, when I took a walk.

Told Prof. Leach (Greek) I thought you might let me come back, and she requested me at once to elect three courses in Greek for next semester. Of course I'm not going to do it, but I'm scared to mention it to her again.

Guess Helen Crosby isn't engaged after all. She is going up to the Yale Prom next week with Gardiner Abbot.

Gertrude has Supper Club tonight. I have it two weeks from tonight, so I'll want a box then.

By the way, will you please send me some of my sleeping-powders? Don't worry about me, as I feel *perfectly well*, and am not worrying about anything, but I just get awake for a few hours in the night.

Mabel sent Cousin Ella some violets for Xmas, and has not heard from her since. Could you tactfully find out whether she ever received them.

With much love, yours<br>Fan

---

January 15

Dearest Mother,

I sent you some roses by express. Hope they reached you safely. Am very glad you are feeling better. Don't overdo when you first go out.

Have decided positively to take: Labor Problems (three

157

hours), and Greek (Aristotle) three hours. Have 6 more hours to choose.

If you are all well, as I'm sure you will be, I would like to bring some of the girls down on Feb. 1st.

Your,

Fan

---

January 16

Dearest Mother,

I think I would like some pictures (just heads) taken in my new white gown with the pearl trimming. Please send the waist to me *today*. The skirt would not be necessary.

Your,

Fan

---

Albany, N. Y.

January 18

Dearest Mother,

Here I am in Albany. Nina, Maude and I arrived here last night. We are to have our pictures taken this morning and go back on the 2.15. Must go to breakfast.

Fan

---

January 19

Dearest Mother,

Mrs. Banks had written and asked us to spend Saturday night with her. We did not want to take the 6.31 Saturday morning (that means getting a carriage to drive to the station), and we thought if we took the 10.26 that it would be impossible to take 6 girls pictures before it got dark. (Three girls backed out at the last minute). So we telephoned to Mrs. Banks and asked her if we could come on Friday late, and have our pictures taken on Sat. Morning. She said yes, and we made all our plans to take the 3.55 on Friday. I went in to ask Mrs. K. and she made an awful row. I talked and talked. Finally I left and later went back again. Miss Cornwall was there. She said that Mrs. K. had left word that I could not go, unless I would not go away between semesters and *even in that case,* she did not want me to go. I said, "I am very sorry, Miss C. but I am going anyway". She gasped, almost fell off her seat, and said, "Even if Mrs. K. does not want you to?" I said "yes" and walked out. A few minutes later a messenger girl knocked at my door and said, "Mrs. K. sent you this". *This* was a leave of absence slip. So she crawled. But I expect I'll have an awful time with her the next time I want to go away.

Mrs. Banks seems very lonesome since Mary got married. Why don't you have her to visit you sometime?

Last night we went over to Prexy's to a reception with food. Prexy was perfectly dandy. We are all crazy about him.

Mother, if you think at all about going away for Easter vacation, and Dad wants me to take a girl with me, I would like so much to take Maude.

Got a note from Charlie Patterson yesterday saying that he had just had his picture taken, and would send me one if I wanted it, and would I please send him one of me. Oh! Law!

Mercy, of course Arthur is engaged to Florence Barbour. What's she doing visiting him all the time, if she isn't. I don't think it's polite. How is Dad? How is the kid?

With love,
Fan

---

January 21

For the love of tripe, Mother, send me some handkerchiefs. I don't know how mine manage to disappear, but it will be disastrous soon, if I don't get some.

Have had the worst time with my room. The steam-pipes froze up and burst on Sunday morning at 6 A.M., and I could not get them fixed until this morning. The room was a perfect refrigerator. This morning there were two men fixing my steam pipes and another mending my shade. But once more order has come out of chaos, and the room is its usual neat self.

Had the dandiest skate this afternoon.

With love,

Fan

---

January 23

Dearest Dad,

Thank you very much for the $20. It arrived quite safely.

I think my pictures are awful. My hair looks as though I had used a curry comb on it. If I look like that, I shall wear a mask in the future.

The Amer. Jour. of Soc. came from Brentano's all right, thank you. You are very sweet to your daughter.

Yours with love,

Fan

---

January 24

Dearest Mother,

Helen, Grace and I will be down on the 7th. The Alumnae luncheon to which the Seniors are invited is on the 8th at Delmonico's. I think it would be fun to have a theatre party Saturday night with Grace's brother, and a friend of his named Allen. (They were both here at Phil.) And we could ask Will Howe.

Yours with love,

Fan

---

January 26

Dearest Mother,

Have been deep in Ethics all day. Skated Friday afternoon and evening and Saturday morning. The boxes of food were something wonderful. Had a party here Saturday night after skating and Supper Club tonight. Thanks for prompt reply to my letter. Will write the men, at once.

With love,
Fan

---

January 27

Mother mine,

Ethics is over. It was not so bad. Rather a nice exam.

Just got a note from Clara Holt. She says her engagement was announced Friday in Claremont and Saturday in Concord. He is a Concord man named Woodworth. (There are getting to be fewer of us L.O.P.H.).

Yes, Wellesley has accepted the challenge.

Yours with love,
Fan

---

January 28

Mother Mine,

Greek is over. It was not so *very* hard, but I did not do well.

Got a letter from Arthur tonight, "breaking the news" of his engagement. It is to be announced on the 8th he said. He told me not to tell Ethel, he would write her himself next week.

Yours,
Fan

---

January 29

Dearest Mother,

No exam today, but have been cramming Art. Will send Mary's letter back to you tomorrow. She wrote me she was going to have a baby (2 or 3 weeks ago). Dear me! it seems strange. Mary! of all people. My friends are certainly distinguishing themselves.

I really don't know what will be playing in New York next week. Get tickets for anything you think is good, *Frocks*

161

and *Frills, The Girl and the Judge, A Message from Mars, The Toreador.* Only NOT *Dolly Varden,* as Helen and Grace saw that in Albany.

Love to Dad and the kid,

Yours,

Fan

---

January 31

Well, Mother mine, exams are over! Hurrah! Nina went to the infirmary yesterday, but is out again today. I don't know just what was the matter with her, sort of a peritonitis attack, I guess.

Mercy! Mother, I don't know any of those people to whose funerals you have been going lately. Pleasant occupation, I must say. I think a trip to Florida would be good for you and Dad. Why don't you go? Next semester I am going to take Greek, Economics, Physiology and Art.

Got a picture of Charlie Patterson this morning. Oh! Mercy!

Dick Day is here for good, staying down at Mrs. Eidel's. I don't know when she is to be married.

Yours-with-love-to-the-family.

Fan

P.S. Hush! speaking of learning anything, Nancy was so stupid at Miss Brown's she couldn't learn anything anywhere.

Never have I seen anything to beat the way the Covells keep moving.

---

February 3

My, Mother, what a horrible Sunday! Rain! Rain! Rain!

Gertrude and I waded to church in town and back (hush! I changed my clothes, when I got in, so I didn't take cold). Jim Davis, Mercer Steele and Billy Carhart were all here yesterday. Today begins my last semester. Oh dear! Oh dear! it is heart-breaking. I love these girls so.

Will *Miss Simplicity* be playing while we are home? The music is very good, they say. For what have you got tickets? Anything will please me.

Well dear, I must go to breakfast.

Your,<br>Fan

---

February 3 — later

Dearest Mother,

Mrs. K. gave me my leave of absence today without a murmur. So Grace, Helen and I will be down on Friday.

Got a note from Brinton Buckwalter today asking me to go to the Yale-Harvard hockey match at the St. Nicholas rink on Feb. 15th. Of course I can't go. I'll have to write him.

The kid wrote me such a dear, sweet, funny letter. Give her a kiss for me. Goodnight.

Fan

---

February 4

Dearest Mother,

The dickens! I just got a special delivery letter from Charlie Bruce saying that neither he nor Mr. Allen can come on Saturday. Isn't that the worst? Will Howe is coming.

So now I have to get two more men. Am I furious? At this late date! Suppose you telephone Ted McGraw. How about Frank Linen? Couldn't you telegraph him signing my name. Guess just the address, Scranton, Pa. would reach him. His name is Frank Insley Linen.

Then there are Joe Scranton, Harry Fisher, or Fred Reynolds to fall back upon, (though I'm not much for having the two latter, and Joe I asked a short time ago).

These men are such bores. I wonder if Frank Janeway would come over from Princeton. No! I won't ask him.

163

Oh! dear, Mammy, I do hate to bother you so, and I always seem to have such mixups.

Charlie I will not have.

I'll write you again when I get time.

Yours,

Fan

---

10.15 P.M. February 8

Dearest Moth.

Arrived quite safely. Found Maude, Nina, and Gertrude in my room. They had lit my gas.

The girls say my laundry is safe. The laundry of those who live on 3rd and 4th is safe, and all the rest was burned.

Goodnight,

Fan

---

February 11

Dearest Mother,

Course I did not mind about you not liking us to be late to breakfast. But in the first place we were not waked up till quarter of nine, then I was bound to take a bath and there was not any hot water, and then Gracie had an awful time with her clothes, and Helen and I waited for her. She looked most uncomfortable at breakfast.

Mammy, do you really think Dad does not want to go abroad? Cause if he does think of it at all, passage ought to be engaged.

Have you new Angelus Music? Ask Dad to please send me the latest lists.

I am sorry that I had to miss this concert. Thank you for the newspaper clipping about Paderewski. All the girls have been talking about how wonderful he was. I am returning the clipping as you asked.

Yours,

Fan

## PADEREWSKI HYSTERICS.

*"Poughkeepsie, N.Y., Friday. — While M. Paderewski was playing in Collingwood Opera House here to-night, before two thousand people, Miss Helen Birdsall Heater, of Waterbury, Conn., a junior at Vassar College, became so enthusiastic while M. Paderewski was playing a nocturne by Chopin that she went into hysterics and screamed wildly. There was a commotion in the audience while the young woman was being carried out. The pianist looked toward the gallery as if annoyed, and the audience broke into tumultuous applause. M. Paderewski turned to his piano, taking in the situation, and played on. He was called out many times and gave three encore numbers after the programme, the last of which was played with his overcoat on, having been called back by the people who lingered."*

---

February 11

Had the most perfect time last night at the Ice Carnival. Skated all the evening, bon-fires, lanterns. There is quite a little snow, but they swept off the ice.

Got a letter from Ethel Boies. She is on her way to San Francisco, sails on the 27th for Japan. Said she had a letter from Arthur, announcing his engagement. She does not seem at all broken-hearted about it.

Tell Dad not to send me too much fruit. Smaller quantities more frequently are better.

Yours with love,
Fan

---

February 14

Dearest Mother,

Miss Leach has said nothing about the Greek scholarship. There is nothing to be said. If I want it, I am to apply.

Mammy, don't breathe a word of this, because not even

165

Grace knows that I know, and *nobody* at all is to know, because I don't believe she'll take it. Grace has been asked to take the scholarship in English!

Mammy, I think it would be dandy for you and the kid and Aunt Mary to come on Feb. 22nd. Maude is a dear to ask you. (You see I have no guest seat for it.) I'll go right down to Mrs. Eidel's and engage rooms today. The kid might stay up and sleep with me. Mercy! she is not made of wax to take cold.

Lovingly,
Fan

---

February 16

Dearest Mother,

Valentine's night we had lots of fun. All the senior tables were decorated with candles, red hearts and candy. When we got to the table, we found that every Senior had a bunch of violets at her place. The sophomores had given them to us, bless their little hearts.

Nina is here shining her shoes. Sweet child, Nina, but a little off.

This morning I was so energetic I got up and stewed some prunes before breakfast and took them to the table.

How is Arthur? Radiant, I suppose. *What about Europe?*

Mabel is feeling pretty well, but she can't come out of the infirmary until the pain in her chest is gone. She has a pain there every breath she takes, and the doctors don't seem able to get rid of it.

Yours,
Fan

---

February 18

Dearest Mother,

I don't know what those crazy kids said to you on the telephone last night. The truth of the matter is this. Honors were given out to our class last night. Eleven got them: Aztell,

Dunham, Heath, Kent, Moore, Johnson, Riblet, Wilson, Hinkle, Orr, Smith. I don't believe you know any of them. Most of them are grinds. There were four honorable mentions: Tanner, Talmadge, Todd, Simpson. The only ones of those you know are the two last. Millicent Todd is in the infirmary with measles, but they sent word over to her.

Phi Beta Kappa is not yet given out. All the honor girls will get it, and *probably* all the honorable mentions. But that is not certain, as one girl last year got honorable mention and not Phi Beta Kappa. So *don't* say that I have Phi Beta Kappa.

Awful storm here yesterday, no trolley cars running. Big fire in Po'keepsie. We kept hearing rumors all day that Smiths had burned. But it turned out to be 2 or 3 stores on Main Street near Smiths.

Mammy, isn't it dandy! And I suppose if I'd been a grind and not been away so much and done so much committee work, I might even have had honors. Just for fun I made a list. I am on the following committees: Committee on Conferring with the Faculty on College Engagements, Fourth Hall Play in 1901 Committee (*As You Like It*), Chairman of Fourth Hall Play (this year — Greek play), Qui Vive, Marshall Club, College Settlement, Vice-President Shakespeare Club, Greek Club, Supiyawlat Club, Vice-President of Phil., Chapter Beta.

Must go to breakfast.

With love,<br>Fan

---

February 19

Dearest Mother,

Enclosed find trip ticket for you to use on Saturday. Did I tell you the play is going to be *She Stoops to Conquer* by Oliver Goldsmith?

Last night the girls at the table gave me a dinner at Smiths. Wasn't that pleasant of them? The class sent all the girls who got anything a white rose, last night, with a card saying "Congratulations from 1902".

But, Mammy, please don't think about Phi Beta Kappa until after it's given out.

With love,<br>Fan

---

February 20

Dearest Dad,

Are you a member of any library in New York? If you are, could you get out these books *at once* and send them to me. They are for the debate girls to use. They will be very careful of them, and return them to you. Now just don't go buy the books, but just tell me whether or not you could get them out of a library. They are:
1. Hilary A. Herbert's "Why the Solid South"
2. Frank W. Gage's "The Negro Problem in the U.S., its Rise, Development and Solution"
3. Philip C. Friese's "The Unconstitutionality of Congressional Action to give Political Power to the Negro in the White Man's Country"
4. W. Cabell Bruce's "The Negro Problem"

The debate is to be on March 22nd. Mabel Day is Chairman, and the question is: "Resolved, that legislation against Negro suffrage is justifiable." Qui Vive has the affirmative, House of Commons, (another club with a secret name) — the negative.

Thank you Daddy mine, with love,

Fan

---

February 20

Dearest Mother,

Think it would make it very pleasant for you to send me some food on Friday. We could have breakfast in my room Sunday morning.

168

Have found out at last what honorable mention means. It is the same as an honor, except that an honor means honor work for all four years and an honorable mention means honor work for Sophomore, Junior and Senior years.

And Mammy, the funny part of it is in my case that I am cock sure I did better work Freshman year than I have ever since. But I guess I don't know.

As regards Phi Beta Kappa, it means *half* your marks are A. (You know they mark you A, B, C, D, and D means flunk.) I don't believe I'll get Phi Beta Kappa.

Mabel came out of the infirmary today. She still has a pain every time she breathes.

Yours with love,<br>Fan

---

February 25

Mammy mine,

More work for the undertaker! The faculty has appointed me a commencement speaker. They appoint six girls out of those who got honors and honorable mentions to make speeches in the chapel at the commencement exercises. We have to write stupid old speeches on stupid subjects and say them off by heart.

Oh! dear! and I believe they have to be in by March. What with that and the Greek play, I'll be a sliver by June.

Must get to work.

With love,<br>Fan

---

February 28

Dearest Mother,

I have the horrible feeling that I *can't stop* from now until June 11th. You have no conception of the amount of work I have to do. Just loads on the Greek play, and the commencement essay. Miss Wylie, (Prof. of English and head of com-

169

mencement essay work) says that we will have to give up our class work, do shabby work the rest of the semester and scrape through examinations. Our essays have to be in, all finished, when we come back from Easter vacation. Then we take elecution lessons from now until June with a woman who comes up from New York. The essays have to be spoken, not read, you know. And anyway I never could write.

I guess after I get started I won't be so discouraged, but they expect so much.

Got a note from Dr. Van de Water congratulating me on having won Phi Beta Kappa. Oh! dear! and it won't be given out for a week or two anyway. Was ever anything more embarassing?

Mammy, for commencement time I have to have: (1) a plain white dress (a wash one I guess) for Bac. Sunday, (2) a *very* light colored or white dress for class day (not a wash dress) and a (3) white graduation dress for commencement day.

There is no getting out of being a speaker. The faculty does not *ask* you, but *appoints* you.

Mammy, my wash came back from the fire this morning. I don't believe I can stand the Troy laundry, everything is so yellow and horrid. Can't I send my wash home? Then it could be mended too. And you could send back cookies with it. If I get a satchel effect like Dad has, it would be quite simple.

The man we get wigs from is Oscar Bermer, 9 West 28th St. I'll do my best to get home on the 7th unless Miss Wylie absolutely forbids it. Shall I bring a girl with me?

With love,<br>Fan

---

March 5

Dearest Dad,

The Junior-Senior debate takes place this month. Gertrude and Grace are on our team. There is a certain legal point

170

in connection with it, upon which they want legal advice (paying for it, of course). Gertrude is going to write Mr. Fred Stimson tonight and ask him for a few minutes appointment on Friday (the 7th). As there would not be time to get his answer before Gertrude would want to leave here Friday morning, *he is to let you know* if he can give her the appointment and what time, and will you please telegraph to her or me collect. In that way all difficulty about his paying for the telegram etc. will be avoided.

I wish she could find out Mr. Choate's opinion on the point in question. Is there any particularly eminent lawyer whose opinion she might be able to find out. Much in regard to the debate rests on the solution of the point in question. I will probably be down on Friday.

With love,<br>Fan

---

March 6

Dearest Mother,

I will take the 11.55 train from here tomorrow. Of course the trains are much delayed now on account of the wash-outs, so I'm very likely to be late. Have you a darned old Guild meeting that afternoon? I'd better go to Mme. Reilley's Friday afternoon and transact my business on Union Square on Saturday. Gertrude is going to New York Friday to see a lawyer and work in the Columbia University library. *She will stay all night with us Friday night.* Guess I'll go up to the library Friday evening and work on my speech.

With love,<br>Fan

---

March 10

Dearest Mother, Got here safely. Cold better. Fourteen girls, including your daughter, got Phi Beta Kappa. Nobody you know. Must stop.

Fan

Dearest Mother,

I do hate to bother you, but couldn't you send me some samples from Siegel, Coopers, Elvicks and Macy's.

Let me explain just what I want. All the actors wear a cotton chiton coming to the knees. The chambry samples sent by Altman's won't do for this. Miss Leach said she thought there were materials sold as cheap woolens, which were sort of cottony (sort of cottony serges). You see it must not be transparent at all. Could you get samples for this?

Then some wear sort of a travelling cloak. The samples of single faced canton flannel will be all right for those.

Then some have large rectangular pieces of goods which they wrap around and around their bodies. The sample of purple cashmere will do for that, but we need other colors and can't afford to spend too much. It must not be transparent, but must be lighter than canton flannel, so that it will wrap around them nicely. Could you try and send me some samples for this?

Mammy, I just hate to bother you so. You are such a love! Must go to dinner, with much love,

Fan

---

Dearest Mother,

I was looking up plays this morning. The only ones with promise seem to be: *Notre Dame, Soldiers of Fortune, The Diplomat, The Modern Magdalene, The Twin Sister, Dolly Varden.*

I don't believe *Her Lord and Master* is good, I don't like Effie Shannon. *The Modern Magdalene* might not be a good one for us to see. DuBarry *certainly* would not, with men along.

Do anything you think best, Mammy.

172

Must study Greek.

With love,
Fan

---

March 19

Dearest Mother,

Busy today. Yesterday was Mabel's birthday. We had a party at the table. If we don't win the debate on Saturday, I think it will kill her.

You do have more trouble with your footmen.

Speech is getting on very slowly and stupidly. I hate it.

Yours,
Fan

---

March 23

Dearest Mother,

It was most pleasant to have you and Dad come up for the debate, but I wish it could have turned out the other way.

The girls have been just as brave as could be about it, but they feel perfectly terrible. You see we lost it last year and to lose it again is mighty hard. I heard that Mabel did not sleep a wink last night. She just got up and lit her gas and sat there. She was dandy to the judges this morning, took them walking, and to chapel and dinner. Grace and Gertrude feel all the worse because they were on last year's debate and lost.

College begins again after vacation on April 9th. That means to get back on the evening of the 8th.

The last day I could apply for a graduate scholarship in Greek is April 9th. So you'd better be thinking about it.

Had the *worst* minister this morning.

Mammy, I can't ask Gertrude to write to Mr. Stimson now. Besides, owing to the fact that it came to her in an envelope addressed by me, she thinks I sent it to her. I guess I'll write him myself. Would that do?

Goodnight. Love to Dad and the kid.
                              Yours,
                                        Fan

---

Dearest Mother,
    Am not getting along at all with my speech, though I
work every minute. I have not written a word. Don't believe
I'll ever finish it.
    Mammy, you are a love about the debate. It means a lot
to us, but it's usually the case that other people don't think so.
Indeed the poor debaters and committee are still sick about it.
    Mammy, we want to send a box of food to the kids who
stay here during vacation.
                              With love,
                                        Fan

---

                                        April 9
Dearest Mother,
    We arrived safely just a few minutes late. I didn't go to
Physiology because it was way over in the lab. and I would
have been late, but I know Mrs. K. will not say anything. I
did go to Economics.
    You and Dad are just dandy, bracing up well.
                              Affectionately,
                                        Fan

---

                                        April 11
Dearest Mother,
    There are several things I want you to send me when my
things come from Mrs. Reilly:
        my pongee dress
        rosebud silk waist
        large pair of scissors
        large and small safety pins
        black and white pins

174

pair of round garters
box of my calling cards (they are in my desk)
envelopes to fit the cards
pair of long shoe strings
soap box (mine was lost in Atlantic City)
I guess that is all. Quite enough isn't it? I would not ask you to send some of these if I had a moment to go to Poughkeepsie.

Mammy, couldn't you send me some addresses where I could write for feathers. I ought to start the head-dresses next week. If you see a rainbow liberty scarf, please buy it for me. One more thing, dear, we want the librettos for the Greek play printed as cheaply as possible. Could Dad send me the addresses of any printers, to whom I could write? Does he have a pull with any?

Say, did Dad mean that about having the girls at the Lake in June? How many and for how long?

Had a note from Edna Le Massena. She is to be married on June 4th. Mother I haven't a friend left who is not married except Ethel, and most of them have children.

With love,<br>Fan

---

April 14

Dearest Mother,

Am so sorry to hear that you have been ill. Do take good care of yourself. Thank you very much for bothering about the things I want. I'll look at the express list on Wednesday.

I'll speak to the girls about June, and we'll arrange about it later. Does Dad think he'll have to be in New York a good deal this summer? I do hope not.

Any color feathers will do, thank you.

Sent in an application for scholarship on Thursday. They'll probably be given out next week. Have not finished my speech yet. Miss Wylie said to bring it in, when I had finished it. She was sweet about it. The essay is going to be bum.

The other speakers are Bessie Davis Wilson ("Ethical Instruction in Elementary Schools"), Elizabeth Moore ("The Isthmian Canal in the Light of Experience"), and Millicent Todd ("The Siamese King and the Siamese People").

Tell the kid "thanks" for her letter. Must stop now.

As ever,

**F.**

P.S. Mammy, just one more thing I wish you'd send me for the play, and that is a *plain little* black carriage parasol. You and Dad are trumps to be so brave. I am crazy about you both. Congratulate the kid on having her tooth out.

---

April 15

Dearest Mother,

For goodness sake, tell me to whom I ought to send Class Day and Commencement invitations. I can have 7 people come to Class Day and 4 to Commencement, and any number of complimentary invitations, (to people you don't expect to come). I'll send one of those to Aunt Mary and Uncle John, for instance. I do hope Aunt Esther will be able to get off from school to come.

So Charlie is going away over the deep. Wonder if he'd like me to write him a steamer letter.

I wouldn't bother Dad about that printer for anything. I just thought he might send me the address of some printer for the libretto. It's just a pamphlet, like any ordinary libretto.

Must stop now. Yours as ever,

Fan

---

April 17

Dearest Mother,

Mabel goes to New York on the 11.25 train tomorrow. She has that pain in her chest again, and is going to see a doctor in New York as soon as she gets there. Then she wants

176

to go up and talk to you, she wants some advice and asked me for it. I told her to go to you for it. On Saturday she is going to Mrs. Young-Fulton's on Union Square, to try and get a position for the summer. Mrs. Y.-F., I am afraid, won't be able to get her anything for the summer unless she keeps it all winter. And she doesn't know whether to get married or not and lots of things. But she'll tell you tomorrow. The poor child is almost crazy and sick besides. Do cheer her up and give her some good advice.

She will be at 988 5th Ave. *about* 4 o'clock Friday afternoon (tomorrow, April 18th). If you won't be home, will you phone me tomorrow about 9.30. Mabel would like you to write a letter about her character to Mrs. M. J. Young-Fulton, and leave it at the house for her, if you are not home.

Mammy, the girls are crazy about you. You're a regular old mother-confessor! Don't say anything about it, but Nina has something awful the matter with her. The doctor thinks it is appendicitis and wants her to go see Dr. Markoe on Saturday the 26th. Nina doesn't want to go alone and would you mind going with her? I'll let you know the time later. Mammy I really think she'll have to have an operation, she's had an awful time with her side and her right leg. We seem to be having our troubles up at old V.C., don't we?

The McCurdys are here now, and I am crazy about them.

Yours with love,
Fan

---

April 18

Dearest Mother,

I am sitting in Nina's room with her. She is in bed writing a letter. The McCurdys went to the theatre with some of the other girls.

Nina told me about today. Poor kid! it's so hard for her. But she's just as brave as she can be about it. You are very

177

sweet to my friends, Mammy dear. I just love you harder than ever.

Mammy, if Mrs. Blackmer comes on won't you sort of look out for her. She knows nothing about New York. And Mammy, when Nina goes down to St. Luke's can't you meet her? She is just crazy about you, as we all are.

Mammy I am going to write to that woman at Simpson-Crawfords for the wings tonight. Mammy, I just hate to bother you, but could you get the enclosed for me some day, when you are in Altman's the first of the week. At least get the same color and kind of material as cheap as you can. We can afford the prices marked on them all right, I guess.

As regards the rainbow samples, I'm afraid none of them will do very well, at least if we can do better. The silk material had too much figure in it and the thin rainbow ribbon had really too faint colors to be seen at any distance whatever.

Thank you dear, so much for all your trouble. I wonder when Nina will get an answer from her mother. I suppose early Sunday morning and then she'd go down on Sunday probably.

Your Fan

---

Friday night

My dearest Mrs. Simpson,

Here I am back again safe and sound but in bed — Fan says she is writing to you, so thought I'd just put in a word or two. The girls are all sweet and insist that they are coming down with me next week. I expect to see a row of tents around the hospital entrance. We were just a minute before time and didn't have any unpleasant waits, we just flew along home. Mrs. Kendrick is very much excited about it all, but what is it to her or to the doctors either for that matter. I hope your second protegée turned out as well as the first, but I don't suppose we shall know until Sunday night. Mrs. Simpson, I just can't tell you how much good you did me — you know, I guess. Thanking you again, your devoted and loving Nina.

---

Dearest Mother,

Nina's mother telegraphed her today to make all arrangements for her operation (I don't think Mrs. Blackmer is coming, as she didn't say anything about it in her telegram.) So Nina wrote to Dr. Markoe. I expect she'll get an answer tomorrow, as she sent the letter special delivery today.

Now she is beginning to think it is wrong for her to have the operation. She thinks it's selfish to give her mother all that worry, when she is not acutely ill, and she thinks she may get better without it. But I don't think she would, Mammy, as she has had that pain for 8 or 9 days and it gets worse every time she walks. She is so plucky that she stands the pain without flinching much, but it's there just the same. The minute she gets the *least bit* tired, it gets so bad she can't stand up. And as long as the doctor advised it, it seems the best thing to be done. Why don't you telephone him and find out if he is going to write her that it is necessary for her to have an operation. She *may* write him that she is much better, but she really isn't.

If Nina goes down on Tuesday, can't you meet her? She'll have the operation on Wednesday, if she goes down on Tuesday. Mammy, won't you go see her and be with her *lots* and be a mother to her.

Mabel came back this afternoon. Haven't had a chance to talk with her yet. I had Supper Club tonight. Such a funny one. We made Welsh rarebit, and fried potatoes and all sorts of messes.

Florence and Isabel are loves. They want me to come to Youngstown in September.

Thank Dad for the printer's address. I'll tend to it early this week. Am still awfully busy.

Mother, I owe old Mary 10c. Please pay her for me, will you?

Jim is here today * * * * * *. He has just gone, and Nina has come in saying that she has no pain at all. Must stop now.

Yours,

Fan

---

2.30 P.M. April 22

Dearest Mother,

Well, I suppose Nina is safely established up at St. Luke's by now. I do hope she will get along all right. What did Dr. Markoe say about her case when you saw him Monday morning?

The graduate scholarships were given out last night and I did not get one. There were not any given to anyone in Greek. Miss Leach is infuriated. I guess it's the easiest solution of my problems, as to whether to come back next year or not.

Haas has not yet sent my shirt waists. Bell has just rung.

Yours,

Fan

---

April 29

Dearest Mother,

Be sure and write us how Nina is every day. And Mammy, ask anybody you think she would like to see to go up there. The aunts, for instance.

You ought to have been here last night. We really celebrated winning the debate against Wellesley. The question was, resolved: "That the United States should Subsidize a Merchant Marine". At 8:30 we formed in a procession outside of Main. We had the three debaters in a cart to which long ropes were attached. About 30 of us pulled it. We had torches and burned red lights, marching all over the campus, singing and shouting. We got out in the circle and made each one of the debaters and the chairman of the committee stand up in

180

the cart, and make a speech. All the college turned out, and there was lots of excitement.

I am enclosing a clipping from the Wellesley newspaper. Vassar picked the subject, and was assigned the negative.

I got the estimates from Miss Gillan. The cheapest was $62.25 and that's without any advertisements in the back. I'm going to have a committee meeting and decide about it.

Hear Ted went up to see Nina yesterday. Six weeks from today is Class Day.

Mother, that man from Simpson-Crawford was perfectly crazy. I ordered: 5½ yards purple, 5½ yards green, 8 yards yellow — He sent: 3½ yards yellow, 3½ yards tan, 5½ yards blue, no purple, no green. Would you do me a favor? Will you send me 4 more yards of yellow. I'll keep the tan because I can use it. If I send back the blue will you change it for purple. I'll send it tomorrow. And send me 5½ yards of green.

Yours,<br>Fan

---

May 4

Mother mine,

Yes, I have all the material I need for the costumes.

We have had the grandest time I ever have had. Of course the weather was dreadful yesterday, but we had the boat ride just the same. My four men were just as nice as they could be. The girls were crazy about them all. I'm so glad Frank came. I do hope he had a good time.

Helen Crum saw Nina. Said she looked sweet. Helen met Aunty Mary, Eloise and Aunt Esther just as she was coming away.

Mammy the box of food was fine.

We are all crazy about the June Lake George house-party. We almost wept at the thought that we had just finished our last Founders. So we're going to have another Founders at the Lake. It would be such fun to have some men up for over a Sunday. Don't you suppose we could arrange it? It would make an awfully big party and the men would have to stay at the hotel, but it's the last time we will all be together. We could have Will, Ted, Fred, Frank, Max, Harry, Mercer, etc. from June 27th to 30th.

I should think we could go to the Lake by the 17th ourselves. I'd like to have Clara Holt and her fiancé.

Fare thee well.

Fan

---

May 6

Mother mine,

Just a line as I'm too busy to think fairly. You said you enclosed a newspaper clipping in your last letter, which you didn't. I wonder if Nina is with you today. Just give her a great big kiss from me, and don't let her come here until she is strong, as she will work hard as soon as she does get here.

We are just calming down after our Founders excitement.

Do you want to come up for the play? It's going to be bum, but I'd like to have you.

I must get to work. Exams begin 2 weeks from Thursday.

Yours,

Fan

---

May 7

Mother mine,

Enclosed find trip ticket. Think it would be fine for you and the kid to come back with Nina. Am busy as a slave.

Yours,

Fan

---

May 8

Dearest Mother,

Am delighted that Nina is getting along so beautifully. Jim couldn't stay away, could he?

182

Am very busy as usual, so will have to close.
Love to Dad, Nina, and the kid. I love them all.

Yours,

Fan

---

May 9

Dearest Dad,

I am just as sorry as I can be about this awful libretto business. I have had my troubles about it this end too. I sent it the first minute I could get it. Miss Leach was awfully slow about it, I kept prodding her up all the time, but it's next to impossible to get anything out of the faculty. I am contrite about Miss Gillan. Please tell her I'm just as sorry as I can be.

Dad, I'm scared to let it go through without seeing the proof. I'll try to get down on Monday afternoon to see it. If I can't do that, can't a special messenger bring it up and take it back that evening? Never mind the cost.

We got $120 worth of ads, so we can pay for it all right. Please send me the name and address of the printer.

Oh! dear! I'm just sick about it. Miss Leach should have had it done before Easter and I should not have been so slow about it myself.

Isn't it pleasant that Nina is able to come back so soon. I'm glad Mother and the kid are coming up with her. Don't be lonesome without them, Daddy dear.

Yours,

Fan

---

May 11

Dearest Mother,

Rehearsal lasted until 5.30. It was the limit, but I don't care. Did the kid get sunburned yesterday? I did, awfully.

Was sorry to have to leave you so suddenly. The kid left her night-robe here.

Dr. Markoe says that Helen will have to be awfully care-

183

ful or she won't graduate. He says she will have to have an operation. With care she needn't have it until summer. Poor kid, she isn't as strong as Nina either. Did you ever know anything like the girls at our table?

Am off to Supper Club.

With love,<br>Fan

---

May 12

Dearest Mother,

Dad is a perfect love to take so much trouble for me. I would never dare let it go through without seeing the proof. I am so glad it is coming up.

Haven't another minute.

With love,<br>Fan

---

May 15

Dearest Mother,

You people had better come up for the play on Friday, as the Sophomore-Freshman basketball game is to be played Saturday morning. What train will you take? Be sure to let me know, and one of the Group will go down and meet you.

Well, I must be off.

Yours,<br>Fan

---

May 20

Dearest Dad,

The librettos were fine, just exactly as I wanted them. They really could not have been better. Thank you so much, Daddy, for all the trouble you took. We never would have had them if it had not been for you. We are coming out all right on the money question, ending up with $130 worth of advertising.

Dad, won't it be fun at the Lake? You are mighty sweet to let me ask all those girls; and the men too for over Sunday at the Sagamore.

I'm so sorry you could not see the play.

Yours with love,

Fan

---

My dear Mother,

Mabel will go to New York on Monday, and stay with you that night. Maybe Tuesday night too. I've set my heart on having Mabel married from the Lake in September. Do persuade her.

Mammy, you must have misunderstood me a lot about invitations. Do let me explain. In the first place, commencement on Wednesday is awfully stupid. It is in the chapel and consists of fool speeches, giving of diplomas, etc. Nobody asks anybody but their own families. The chapel is always hot and each girl gets four invitations. On my four I will have you, Dad, the kid and Aunt. *No one else.* I wouldn't have Dr. Stires there for the world! What did you ask him for? It's admittedly the stupidest thing we have during the entire week. I wouldn't have him come down from the Lake for that for anything. It would be stupid for him, and *I would hate it.* On the contrary *I want him* on the 9th and 10th. So I'll have to write him I guess, and explain your mistake. The 9th and 10th *are fun.* Besides I have no seat for him on the 11th. And speaking of ministers, I want him and Dr. and Mrs. Van de Water to be here surely for the Dickens-Shakespeare boat ride *Monday afternoon,* the 9th. That's about the most fun of all.

*Be sure* you don't forget your "present at the door" cards. They're most important.

Thanks for the food. Isn't it *Hot?*

Yours,

Fan

185

Sunday A.M.

For goodness sake, Mother, send me all my short white piqué skirts. (Those which are too short for me, I'll give to Phebe, our little table maid who has been ill.) Also one long piqué skirt and my two mercerized cotton sailor suits and the trees for my shoes (the last I left home when I was there to see Nina). Could you get them off in tomorrow's express?

There is a Miss Malin here visiting Fallie McKinley. She knows H. Warren, was in that opera. Helen met the man in September. He grew madly crazy about her and they got engaged. He is of fine family, has not a cent, and he is a physician with no practice. Philadelphians think he has fallen into a snap. He is a musical genius and crazy about music. He is slight, not very tall, brown eyes and hair, and a winning smile. His manner is brusque, rude at times, but he is a fine fellow.

The Juniors took us Seniors out on the river last night from 6.30 to 11. It was perfectly beautiful and cool.

Got a note from Clara Holt. She can come to the Lake. Hurrah!

Must go to breakfast.

Yours,<br>Fan

---

May 29

Mother mine,

As my plans are now, I think I'll go to New York Monday on the 1.05 train, have Mrs. Newton manicure my nails that afternoon and that evening try on and decide about summer clothes. (The box came all right, but of course it has been cool ever since it came.) Then Tuesday morning I can go to Duponts and have my picture taken, and do my other shopping. Tuesday afternoon the girls can come down, and Wednesday we can come back to college.

What about the girls coming down on Tuesday anyway? Dad told me to invite them all, but how are you going to have room? You see, there are ten at the table, Clara Holt will be here, Frances' sister Margery (a perfect dear) is here, and Dick. Do tell me what to do.

Well, au revoir, Yours,

Fan

---

Mother mine,

You are sort of crazy. Last night I got a letter addressed:

Miss Helen Simpson
Vassar College
Poughkeepsie, N. Y.

in your hand writing. I shipped it on to the kid at once.

Have secured a Class Day seat for Nanna, and think I can get her one for commencement. Aunt Esther writes that she will try to get up to Pok. by 4 o'clock on Tuesday. If she only could get the 1 o'clock train from New York, it would be fine. I'll be sick if she doesn't.

Frank Linen can't get away from the bank the last week in June and the last week in July. Isn't that a shame? I'll talk to you about it on Monday. My plans for commencement week are as follows:

Monday — 3 o'clock boat ride; evening, Phi Beta Kappa.

Tuesday — 4 o'clock, Class Day etc.; evening reception etc. (Piano used for Class Day, have engaged Vossler to pack it that afternoon, as soon as Class Day exercises are over.)

Wednesday — morn. Commencement; afternoon (have engaged Baker to come out and pack sheep picture).

Wednesday — evening class supper.

Thursday — morning (have engaged Lucky Platt to come get furniture and pack it.)

Please ask Dad about sending the things by freight to 988 or 97 Fifth.

Guess I'll try to engage a woman to pack my things Wed-

187

nesday afternoon and Thursday. Then maybe I can get home Thursday night or Friday morning early.

I am sick about that other wig. I'll do my best to find it myself, and pay for it myself if I can't find it. Did he ask anything extra for keeping the other one so long?

Mammy dear, Maude and I are just sick. Phil. is $30 deficient. Isn't that awful? Do you suppose Dad would lend me that, and then as soon as he gave me my own money in September, I would return it. Or he could give it to me for a graduation present, and give me nothing else.

My Class Day guests are as follows:
1. Mother
2. Father
3. Helen
4. Dr. Van de Water
5. Mrs. Van
6. Dr. Stires
7. Aunt Esther?

On Gertrude's invitations which she has given me
8. Mrs. Banks?
9. Frances S., Anne K., Helen H. or Mabel L.?

On Ellen Cobb's invitation, which she has given me
10. Nanna

My commencement guests are as follows:
1. Mother
2. Father
3. Helen
4. Aunt ES.

On Nina's invitation which I think I can secure
5. Nanna

Must go to lunch.

Yours with love,<br>Fan

Gee! this is a whopper of a letter!

## ARISTOTLE'S IDEA OF DEMOCRACY

A democratic form of government is one in which the freemen must be sovereigns. Aristotle further explains his definition of democracy by saying that the free population must be numerous and decidedly in the majority. They must be the poor as distinguished from the rich aristocracy, not the poverty-stricken, however. Rather what we term the "middle class." Only in fulfilling these conditions can a government be made good and lasting. This must exclude all slaves and foreign artisans in the state, for Aristotle considered all foreigners inferior to the Greeks and slaves decidedly ignoble. The people should have leisure, in this ideal democracy, but not idleness; they should cultivate the mind and attend to the government. Many ask by what democracy exists, by what right the mass is sovereign? One idea was that all men were born equally free, therefore should have equal share in the ruling. A later principle was that men should have a voice in governing in proportion to the services they had rendered the state. This is the principle of contribution. Others said a large body was less easily corrupted or moved by passions and therefore more fit to rule. Aristotle said that for this form of government to succeed the citizens must have a high average of intelligence and virtue. In any case it is very apt to become corrupt. The "demos" should be judged according to its use or abuse of power. It is perverted when its magistrates seek their own good and not that of the people.

Some of Aristotle's principles are still applicable; the most important one is the distinction between government for the good of the people and for the good of the rulers.
*Poughkeepsie Daily Eagle,* June 12, 1902.

## AFTER COLLEGE

On board S.S. Fanita cruising
from Bolton Landing to Rogers
Rock, Saturday evening
September 16, 1905

Mother darling,

I love you. You are a trump.

We got all the confetti off as soon as we got on board and are all straight again. It is so very light on the lake and not at all cold. Our trunks and suit cases seem to be untouched. Of course no one will know that we are a bride and groom!

Ed and I both send our courteous greetings to all, and thanks for coming to our wedding. And we especially thank you and Dad for everything, including the glorious house-party of this last week. Also Mother and Father Townsend for their so generous wedding present of our up-coming trip abroad.

Especial love to the maid-of-honor, bridesmaids, best man, ushers, family of the groom and of the bride.

I just *love* Ed. Ed just *loves* me. We are very happy.

Always your loving daughter<br>Fan Townsend

---

*The following letter is from Gertrude Barnard Townsend (pregnant). She was one of the 1902 "group." She came to the wedding and houseparty in 1905, and ended up marrying the best man, Myron Townsend, brother of Ed.*

New York City<br>October 2, 1908

Bless your heart, Fanny dear, and the very warmest congratulations. A daughter! Your mother was so full of happy news when she came in today—I think I have never seen her so elated. And it was splendid to hear all about you and my dear little new niece.

A regular Christmas box appeared this morning. I was delighted to see your good looking coat, and can't resist accepting the loan, though I'm afraid Myron only half approves of such a maneuver. It will be so nice to have it.

The little smocked dress is a darling one, and I hope before very long to have little cousin to adorn it. Where did you find such a lovely one, Fan dear? The babe is certainly rich tonight, with her beautiful afghan too.

Myron and I are very much pleased that you celebrated our anniversary by the coming of little Frances. And what a dear thoughtful sister you are to order those gorgeous dahlias for us. I don't know when I have seen any more exquisite flowers. They seem made for the rooms, so harmonious are they, and we have been thoroughly enjoying them. Thank Ed for us too.

I want you to know, my dear, how constantly my thoughts

are with you, and how very happy I am for you. I do feel we have many joyous times in store for us together with our children. Frances' arrival has made me look forward so eagerly, trying to predict an event three weeks away.

A heartfull of love, Fanny, sister o' mine, and so many thanks for all your thoughtfulness.

Gertrude

*Frances' arrival, mentioned in the letter above, evidently satisfied her mother's wishes for a family since no other children were born. No longer concerned with lining up boys for theatre parties and dances, and secure in her marriage, Fan turned her attention to philanthropy, as every well-bred and amply provided for woman did. The following letters indicate her involvement during World War I as head of the Vassar College Unit which aided the French War Relief.*

---

SOCIÉTÉ FRANCAISE
DE SECOURS AUX BLESSÉS MILITAIRES
(Croix Rouge Française)

Paris, France
le 2 Novembre 1920

Madame,

Nous avons le grand plaisir de vous adresser la médaille commémorative 1914-1919 comme témoignage de reconnaissance pour les services que vous avez rendus à notre Société en l'aidant dans l'assistance aux enfants de la ville de Verdun.

Et nous vous prions d'agréer nos sentiments de gratitude.

Le President
G. Pay

Mrs. Edward Townsend
Présidente du Vassar Collège Unit

192

"GOUTTE DE LAIT ET DISPENSAIRE" S.B.M.
Oeuvre Luxembourgeoise & Hollandaise
Fondation Américaine du Vassar Unit

Verdun (Meuse, France)
le 14 Janvier, 1921

Madame Townsend, Edouard
Présidente du Vassar Collège Unit

Madame,

Il nous est agréable de vous annoncer que par ce même courrie nous vous adressons, sous pli séparé et recommandé, La médaille commémorative de la Grande Guerro en souvenir du secours que vous avez apporté aux populations malheureuses de Verdun et de la région.

Ce simple témoignage de reconnaissance de la Croix Rouge FRANCAISE est bien peu; Mais, il nous reste chez nous Verdunois et Français un témoignage autrement élevé: celui du souvenir durable que vous nous avez laissé.

Veuillez MADAME, reçevoir l'expression de nos sentiments de bien vive sympathie et d'éternel souvenir.

La Directrice             Le President

*Even before Fan's work in the French War Relief had ended, she joined the Young Women's Christian Association and thereupon, during the rest of her life dedicated much of her time and energy to the work of this organization. From 1917 when she first joined until the time she resigned shortly before her death, the "Y" was her dominant interest outside her home, as the following resolution, adopted April 21, 1970, indicates so well.*

Central Branch
# THE YOUNG WOMEN'S CHRISTIAN ASSOCIATION OF THE CITY OF NEW YORK
Resolution in Honor of Mrs. Edward Perry Townsend
Presented by Mrs. Edward T. Hetzler

The Committee of Management has granted me the great pleasure of bringing to its attention a matter concerning a most kindly and most astute "young woman," whom I have known many years, Mrs. Edward Perry Townsend.

I like to think that our paths first crossed in 1902, for it was in that year that I was born and that Fanny graduated from Vassar, with my favorite Aunt Evelina Pierce as a classmate. Both women have shared a life-long interest in the education and welfare of young women and girls.

In truth, however, it was in the early thirties, during those years known as The Depression, that as a younger woman, I became interested in the YWCA in New York, and came to know Fanny well, and to love and respect her. She demonstrated a complete grasp of the problems with which it was trying — and is still trying to cope.

Mrs. Edward Perry Townsend joined the Young Women's Christian Association in 1917, thereafter showing a devotion to the organization which in warmth of understanding and length of service is hardly to be matched. She became a member of the Board of Directors of the YWCA of the City of New York in 1919, serving on many of the committees of that Board. She was President of this Board from 1944 to 1948. Her fiftieth anniversary as a member of the YWCA was honored by a special citation in 1967. She was elected an Honorary Member of the Board of Directors of the YWCA of the City of New York in January of 1970. Late in her YWCA career she joined us at Central Branch as a leader, a guide, and a very dear friend.

Therefore, I offer the following resolution for approval by the Committee of Management of Central Branch of the YWCA of the City of New York

*Resolved,* That Mrs. Edward Perry Townsend be unanimously elected as an Honorary Member of this Committee of Management of Central Branch, YWCA of the City of New York, and that this official act, together with this statement of our most affectionate regards for Mrs. Townsend, be recorded in the minutes of this meeting; and further, that copies of this resolution be sent to Mrs. Townsend and members of her family.

*To complete the story it should be mentioned that Helen, "The Kid," graduated from Vassar in 1912, never married but made numerous friends on the tennis courts where she distinguished herself as an excellent player. She lived most of her life at Lake George where she dedicated herself to town affairs and was especially active on the Board of Education.*

*"The Kid" died in March, 1973 and with the sale of her home during the following summer, the last of the Simpsons disappeared from Lake George which had known them well for more than three quarters of a century.*

# EPILOGUE

*Had I found and read these letters before my mother's death in 1970, it would have been "most pleasant." Unfortunately I did not even know of their existence until I emptied the New York apartment where she had lived for the last forty-seven years of her life.*

*Had I read them while I was at Vassar, I would have enjoyed my "French Leaves" with a freer conscience, and I might have dared to ask my Mother to do more errands for me.*

*Had my children read them, they might have gone to Vassar. They would never have believed that their grandmother could sew a corset cover, make fudge, or need help from HER mother in making decisions. We all thought of her as a truly "Able General," an efficiency expert, an enthusiastic hostess, a completely compassionate and generous person, and always a loyal member of her Vassar Group.*

*In fact, Mother was a pippin!*

Weston, Vermont
October, 1973

turn of *the* century

# THE GROUP

*an*
*album*

*Papa*

"*One of the most distinguished men in the music trade is Mr. John Boulton Simpson, the millionaire.*"

*Mama*

"*Between
running almost
daily errands for
Fan she served
as treasurer of St.
Andrew's Guild
and manager of
St. Luke's
Home.*"

*The Shelton Sisters Reunited (Mama at left) 1898*

*Cousin Robert and Ella*

*The "Kid" (Atlantic City)*

*"Fanny's mother, Frances, was one of eight children who became orphaned when both parents died of pneumonia within two days."*

*Fanny/Freshman at Vassar*

"*I do want to set your mind at rest by telling you that I am beautifully fixed.*"

*Lake George House party during college days*
*Fanny - second from left at top*
*Papa - top right*

"I'd like to have
a houseparty
with Ethel Boies,
Anne K. and
some Princeton
men."

*Papa (extreme left) hosts a picnic at Lake George...*

*...and Mama & Papa entertain some of the Aunts & friends*

"The Simpsons were one of the leaders of the social set at Lake George."

*Papa's steam yacht "Fanita" on Lake George*

*\* Does friend feel sick?*

*Above - corner of "Fanita" main cabin / At right - Mama and Papa on deck with a friend \**

"Even if some of the summer crowd has gone we could go out on the 'Fanita.'"

"Nirvana"

Mama in the garden / "Nirvana"

"I can hardly
wait to join you
and the others at
'Nirvana' after
college closes."

*Papa's study*

*Fanny's bedroom*

*The playhouse
(the "Kid" at left)*

*"Nirvana"*

"Yesterday Papa
sent me a sample
of wall paper
from Lake
George. I would
like to plan my
room myself."

Fanny / Pre-marriage, 1905

"I just LOVE
Ed. Ed just
LOVES me."

*The Wedding Party / Lake George. 1905*

*Family Gathering*

"*Ed and I both send our courteous greetings to all and thanks for coming to our wedding.*"

The Happy Moment
from left - the bride and groom, the "Kid", Myron Townsend
and Louise Townsend Coulter

"*Especial love to the maid-of-honor, bridesmaids, best man, ushers, family of the groom and of the bride.*"

*Regatta at the Sagamore, Lake George*

*Papa's "Grand Pierce" / The "Kid" at the wheel*

*" 'The Kid' lived
most of her life
at Lake George."*

*Congratulating J. C. Penny on his 90th birthday Fanny still loved hats!*

"*Fanny's work at the 'Y' brought her into contact with many notables.*"

THE YOUNG WOMEN'S CHRISTIAN ASSOCIATION
OF THE CITY OF NEW YORK

To *Mrs. Edward Perry Townsend*
In her Fiftieth Year of Service

For her interest in all activities that build and
advance the growth of the YWCA, and
❖ for the high level of her leadership as a
worker in these activities ◆—◆—◆

But primarily for her ability and readiness to
search out the answers, to adapt to change,
❖ and to remain objective on questions of
deep personal concern ◆—◆—◆

We, the Board of Directors, take pride in honoring you on
the occasion of the Annual Luncheon on October 17, 1967.

*"The 'Y' to
which she gave
more than fifty
years of service
was her dominant
interest outside
her home and
family."*